SELECT WINNING STOCKS USING TECHNICAL ANALYSIS

D1603692

SELECT WINNING STOCKS USING TECHNICAL ANALYSIS

CLIFFORD PISTOLESE

McGraw-Hill

New York Chicago San Francisco
Lisbon London Madrid Mexico City
Milan New Delhi San Juan Seoul
Singapore Sydney Toronto

1 2 3 4 5 6 7 8 9 0   AGM/AGM   0 9 8 7 6

ISBN-13: 978-0-07-147814-4
ISBN-10: 0-07-147814-0

This publication is designed to provide accurate and authoritative information in regard to the subject matter covered. It is sold with the understanding that neither the author nor the publisher is engaged in rendering legal, accounting, futures/securities trading, or other professional service. If legal advice or other expert assistance is required, the services of a competent professional person should be sought.

—From a Declaration of Principles Jointly Adopted by
a Committee of the American Bar Association and
a Committee of Publishers

McGraw-Hill books are available at special quantity discounts to use as premiums and sales promotions, or for use in corporate training programs. For more information, please write to the Director of Special Sales, Professional Publishing, McGraw-Hill, Two Penn Plaza, New York, NY 10121–2298. Or contact your local bookstore.

This book is printed on acid-free paper.

Library of Congress Cataloging-in-Publication Data

Pistolese, Clifford.
    Select winning stocks using technical analysis / by Clifford Pistolese.
        p. cm.
    ISBN 0-07-147814-0 (hardcover : alk. paper)
    1. Investment analysis. 2. Stocks—Prices. I. Title.
    HG4529.P57 2007

    332.63'2042—dc22

2006015491

I dedicate this book to my sisters-in-spirit, Dr. Marlene Lengner and Dr. Loretta Trautman. With their consistent support and appreciation, I have been able to maintain the motivation and strength to make sure my wife is well cared for in her nursing home. If I were to pass on before her, I'm confident they would ensure that Ramona continues to get the warm and loving attention she deserves.

CONTENTS

List of Illustrations   xiii

Preface   xv

Chapter 1

Where Is Your Broker's Loyalty?   1

Introduction   1
Customer Beware   2
Questions about Commissions   2
Trading on Margin   3
Risks of Selling Short   3
Discretionary Accounts   3
Making Decisions Independently   4

Chapter 2

Technical View of the Market   5

Introduction   5
Market Phases   5
Charting Market Phases   6
Tops and Bottoms   7
Pattern Variations   12
Charts of Market Indexes   12
Adapting to Market Phases   13

Chapter 3

Riding the Bull   15

Introduction   15
Investing Aggressively   15
Analyzing Stock Price Patterns   16
Stock Prices and Moving Averages   17
Fundamental Analysis   23
Assessing Risk   24

Chapter 4

A Balancing Act   25

Introduction   25
Adjusting Your Portfolio   25
Closed-End Funds   26
Real Estate Investment Trusts   28
Trading for Capital Gains   30

Chapter 5

Defeating the Bear   33

Introduction   33
Recognizing a Top   34
Technical Indicators   34
Economic Signs   35
Signals from Commodities   35
Cyclical Industries Decline First   35
Preserving Your Capital   35
Suggested Portfolio Content   38

Chapter 6

Picking Winners in the Stock Market   41

Introduction   41
Picking Short-Term Winners   42
Picking Intermediate-Term Winners   46
Checking Risk versus Return   48

Investing for Income   48
Review and Preview   51

Chapter 7

Golden Opportunities   53
Introduction   53
Gold Bullion   54
Exchange-Traded Gold Funds   54
Mining Gold   55
Hedged Gold Sales   55
Potential Risks   56
About Mining Companies   56
A Selection of Companies   56
Decision Considerations   58
Tracking a Gold Fund   59

Chapter 8

Diversifying to Limit Risk   61
Introduction   61
Diversifying among Stocks   61
Index Funds   62
Mutual Funds   62
Closed-End Funds   62
Notes and Bonds   63
Real Estate   63
Precious Metals   64
Cash Equivalents   64
Diversification Considerations   64
A Sample Diversified Portfolio   65

Chapter 9

Stocks to Buy and Hold   69
Introduction   69
Stock Selection Guidelines   69

Stock Selection Procedure   72
Selecting Companies   73
How to Follow Up   85

Chapter 10

Pitfalls to Avoid   87

Introduction   87
Tactical Pitfalls   88
Buying Near the Top   88
Buying a Flat Liner   88
Trading the Tape   89
Trading Frequently   89
Buying Penny Stocks   90
Borrowing Money   90
Selling Short   90
Trading "at the Market"   90
Buying on Tips   91
Buying on Media Hype   91
Buying on the Phone   92
Buying on Rumors   92
Buying on Consensus Opinion   93
Buying on Message Board Comments   93
Buying What You Don't Understand   93
Trading Emotionally   94
Assessing Risk Tolerance   95

Chapter 11

Becoming a Self-Directed Investor   97

Introduction   97
Finding a Full-Service Broker   98
Making the Transition   99
Internet Brokerages   99
Staying with Your Current Broker   100
Rewards of Self-Direction   101

Chapter 12

Review Exercise   103

    Introduction   103
    Making Capital Gains   103
    Which Stocks to Avoid?   119
    Which Stock Has More Potential?   133
    Choosing the Right Time Frame   141
    Assessing Risk   149

Appendix A. Sample Stock Portfolio   157

Appendix B. Glossary   159

Appendix C. Helpful Web Sites   171

Appendix D. Bibliography   181

Note to Reader   183

Index   185

LIST OF ILLUSTRATIONS

Chart 2-1   Market Goes through Bull and Bear Phases

Chart 2-2   Market Is Range Bound

Chart 2-3   Head and Shoulders

Chart 2-4   Rounding Top

Chart 2-5   Double Top

Chart 2-6   Inverted Head and Shoulders

Chart 2-7   Rounding Bottom

Chart 2-8   Double Bottom

Chart 3-1   Ideal Stock Price and Moving Average Relationship

Chart 3-2   Acceptable Stock Price and Moving Average Relationship

Chart 3-3   Minimally Acceptable Stock and Moving Average Relationship

Chart 3-4   Unqualified by Falling Price

Chart 3-5   Unqualified by Flat Price

Chart 3-6   Unqualified by Low Angle of Ascent

Chart 3-7   Riding a Parabolic Price Curve

Chart 4-1   Making Capital Gains in a Trading Range

Chart 6-1   Stock Price Moves Up through Moving Average

Chart 6-2   Stock Price Stays above Moving Average

Chart 6-3   Stock Price Falls through Moving Average

Chart 9-1   Ideal Stock Price and Moving Average Relationship for Buy and Hold Investor

Chart 9-2   Acceptable Stock Price and Moving Average Relationship for Buy and Hold Investor

Chart 9-3   When to Sell a Long-Term Holding

PREFACE

The key to selecting winners in the stock market is finding stocks that are in strong uptrends that can produce large capital gains. This book reveals a visual method for identifying these powerful uptrends in stock price charts you generate on your computer. You will also learn ways to determine when an uptrend has lost its momentum and identify the point where a stock should be sold. Charts that contain this crucial information can be made at no cost from certain Internet Web sites. Since the charts show current data taken directly from the stock market, your transactions can be made in a timely fashion.

By following the evaluation procedures outlined in this book, you can select your investments and you won't be misled by a stockbroker who lacks competence or integrity. Selecting your own stocks allows you to keep commission costs low by using a deep discount brokerage. Doing independent research also enables you to find stocks not yet discovered by other investors, which means you can buy at low prices.

There are times when the recommendations given by a full-service broker are untrustworthy. This can happen if a broker is pressured to sell underwritten or sponsored stocks the firm has in inventory. In this situation the purchase of a stock directly from a brokerage produces income for the company and a commission for the broker, but the stock may not be a suitable investment for you. Also, when a broker is trying to achieve a monthly sales quota, he or she may urge you to act too hastily. But the most widespread and detrimental mismatch of interests is when a broker's primary objective is to earn commissions and finding the most appropriate investment for you is a secondary consideration.

Perhaps you have an account at an Internet brokerage. If you do, the analytical techniques explained in this book provide several important advantages. First, you will learn how to select stocks that can make large capital gains. Second, you will be able to recognize the signal that a stock should be sold. Third, you will not need to purchase a premium trading platform service. Fourth, and most important, you will be able to take charge of your financial future by using the free resources of the Internet to apply the tactics that are outlined in this book.

Whether you are working with a full-service broker, an Internet brokerage, or both, this book will help you select profitable investments, keep costs to a minimum, and make sure your own interests receive top priority.

Here is an overview of the topics to be covered. Chapter 1 helps you evaluate your relationship with your current broker. Chapter 2 provides an overview of technical analysis and presents stock price charts to help you identify major bullish and bearish trends in the market. Chapters 3, 4, and 5 describe how to readjust your portfolio for bull, range-bound, and bear market phases. Chapter 6 explains how to use the free technical analysis resources available on the Internet to pick stocks that can achieve major gains in less than a year. The easily recognized stock price patterns that identify these high-performance stocks are illustrated and explained in this chapter. Chapter 7 considers how to invest in gold for protection against inflation, international confrontations, governmental fiscal mismanagement, terrorism, pandemics, and other natural disasters. Chapter 8 indicates how to diversify your investments to control the level of risk. Chapter 9 provides a list of companies in essential businesses. They increase their earnings based on effective business models, experienced management, and the ability to compete successfully. These are companies whose stocks you can buy and hold for long-term capital gains. Chapter 10 identifies common investment pitfalls and indicates how to avoid them. Chapter 11 describes how to leave a broker who may be incompetent or unethical and find a new broker who will respect your independent decision making. Chapter 12 is a review exercise to help assess your ability to use technical analysis to select stocks capable of major capital gains.

1

WHERE IS YOUR BROKER'S LOYALTY?

INTRODUCTION

This chapter describes some of the common problems in the relationships between brokers and investors. If you have ever used a full-service broker, you might be familiar with some of these issues. Brokers are compensated by earning commissions on customers' transactions, and the basic function of a broker is that of a sales representative. As a sales person, the broker's primary objective is to generate a large number of transactions, and the appropriateness of each trade for a particular customer is sometimes a secondary consideration. Consequently, the payment system of many brokerage firms produces a mismatch between what is good for the brokerage and what would be best for the investor.

This problem occurs when the brokerage has underwritten an issue of stock and has a large inventory of it to sell. In this situation many brokers feel pressured to sell their quota of shares both to please their brokerage firm and to get the commissions. When forced to chose between selling brokerage sponsored stocks and funds and selling what is suitable for a particular customer, many brokers submit to the pressure from management and sell the brokerage endorsed investments.

CUSTOMER BEWARE

If you are a client of a full-service brokerage, your net worth is subject to losses if your broker gives you poor advice. To provide sound advice, your broker should be aware of your financial assets, investment objectives, financial need, and tolerance for risk. Did your broker discuss these matters with you thoroughly? Can you depend on him or her to select stocks and other investments that are suitable for you? If you are a conservative investor, has your broker suggested investing in high-risk stocks and not warned you about the potential downside? Has your broker convinced you to buy stocks that resulted in losses? Has your broker sold you brokerage sponsored mutual funds that have performed worse than the market averages? If you need reliable income flow, has your broker found stocks that pay high dividends and offered them to you? If you are risk averse, has your broker suggested how you might diversify your portfolio to reduce the level of risk? These are a few of the questions and issues to consider when deciding if your broker has been providing good service.

QUESTIONS ABOUT COMMISSIONS

Has your broker ever given you a schedule of commission rates so you can see in advance how much a purchase or sale is going to cost? Do you feel the brokerage commissions are too high? Has your broker ever been willing to negotiate commission charges? If you are an active trader, has your broker ever voluntarily reduced a commission to show appreciation for the amount of business you give to him or her?

When your broker recommends an investment, do you feel pressured? If your broker has asked you to trade in and out of stocks frequently, have you wondered whether his or her motivation might be to get the commissions? If you have been with your broker for a long time, has the value of your portfolio increased a satisfactory amount? If you have been with a full-service brokerage and you are not satisfied with the answers to these questions, you have sufficient reason to move your account to a different brokerage.

TRADING ON MARGIN

If you are on margin now or have thought about using it in your stock market dealings, you should be aware of the costs and the risks. When you borrow money from the brokerage to trade stocks, you must pay interest on the loan. If you buy a stock on margin and it goes down beyond the limit established by the brokerage, your broker will notify you to deposit more money in the account. If you can't do that, the brokerage can force you to sell some of your holdings to protect their investment in the stock. They can also do this without notifying you if you cannot be reached. In that situation, the broker can sell your stock and you must take the loss. If you now have a margin account, it is prudent to convert it to a cash account before the next bear market arrives. Meanwhile, try to reduce the amount of debt in your account.

RISKS OF SELLING SHORT

If you have a margin account, your broker may let you borrow some shares to sell short. Selling short is one of the riskiest tactics an investor can use. If you short a stock at $10 and it goes to $20, your loss is 100 percent. If it goes higher, there is no limit on how much you can lose. A broker who encourages you to sell short is letting you engage in a high-risk transaction. If you now have a short position in any stock, watch it carefully and cover it before a substantial loss develops.

DISCRETIONARY ACCOUNTS

In a discretionary account, the investor gives the broker the authority to trade on his or her own initiative. It is very tempting to some brokers to make frequent trades for the purpose of generating commissions. If you have a discretionary account and the broker has been trading excessively without proportionate profits for the number of transactions, you should tell the broker to switch you into a cash account.

MAKING DECISIONS INDEPENDENTLY

This book will provide guidance on how to do research on the Internet so you will not need to depend on suggestions from a broker. You will also learn how to analyze price charts to help you select stocks and other investments. After you learn the basics of technical analysis, you can be a self-directed investor and free yourself from relying on a broker who has a conflict of interests. The chapters that follow will provide information, procedures, and research sources on the Internet to help you become independent and take control of your financial future.

2

TECHNICAL VIEW OF THE MARKET

INTRODUCTION

The stock market is like the Rorschach inkblot test in which people see what they are inclined to see. Some investors look at the market, focus on the positive elements, and are convinced it will go up. Others concentrate on the negative aspects and believe it will go down. Eventually, the market reveals which group was right and which was wrong. Rather than engage in this subjective evaluation, many investors use more objective methods to take one side or the other. One effective approach now being used by investors to review the status of the market is called *technical analysis*. This chapter provides charts to illustrate some of the common price patterns and explains how they can be analyzed to identify the various phases of the market.

MARKET PHASES

The stock market is usually in one of three phases.

1. In the bullish phase, the market is in a long-term trend upward, and downward price movements are relatively short in duration.

2. In the bearish phase, the market is in a long-term down-trend, and upward price movements are relatively short in duration.

3. In the range-bound phase, the market moves sideways, and prices fluctuate within a relatively narrow vertical distance.

Note: The patterns in this book have been idealized for the purpose of clarity. Actual stock price patterns will not be as well defined. For this reason, considerable practice is necessary to become skilled at the art of chart interpretation.

CHARTING MARKET PHASES

See Chart 2-1. In the bullish phase, the uptrend is identified by a series of rising bottoms. In the bearish phase, the downtrend is defined by a series of descending tops.

CHART 2-1

Market Goes through Bull and Bear Phases

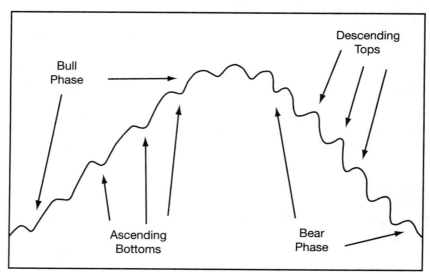

CHART 2-2

Market Is Range Bound

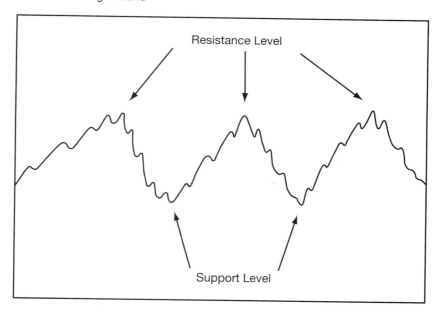

Refer to Chart 2-2. Note the continuing fluctuations between the top and bottom of the range. Range-bound markets usually occur as a temporary phase in a long-lived bull market. When a range-bound condition develops, long-term investors continue holding stocks in anticipation of the next move to the upside. After the top and bottom of the range have been established, some short-term investors buy low and sell high within the range.

TOPS AND BOTTOMS

When the market is in a bullish phase, many stocks are showing large capital gains, and investors wanting to take those gains try to determine when a bull market is topping out. Charts 2-3, 2-4, and 2-5 show three common price patterns that often appear at the top of bull markets.

CHART 2-3

Head and Shoulders

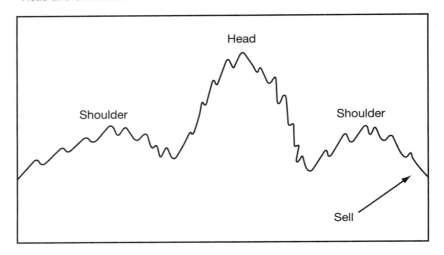

Refer to Chart 2-3. This topping out pattern is a crude outline of a head and shoulders. This is one of the patterns that may occur after a bull market has run its course. The time to sell is when the descent from the shoulder on the right has developed into a downtrend with two or more declining short-term tops.

Refer to Chart 2-4. This rounding top pattern is another way a bull market may end. While the rounding top is being formed, knowledgeable investors who have been holding stocks realize the stocks have become overpriced. They sell their stocks to enthusiastic buyers who are still willing to pay high prices. This top forms as the stockholders distribute their shares to the buyers. Gradually the relationship shifts from an excess of buyers driving prices up, to an excess of sellers driving prices down. The time to sell is during the final stage of the distribution process after a downtrend has been established.

Refer to Chart 2-5. The double top is another pattern that signals the end of a bull market. After the first top forms, investors can see what the highest price was. When the price rises to that level

CHART 2-4

Rounding Top

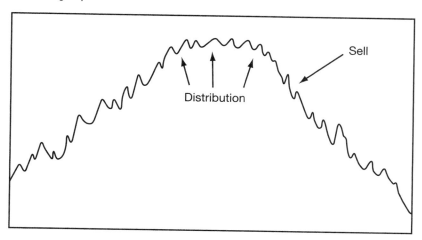

CHART 2-5

Double Top

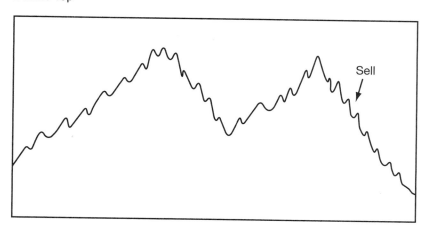

again, many of the remaining stockholders are eager to sell. The selling increases and develops downward momentum and a bear market begins. The time to sell is after two descending short-term tops have appeared as the price declines from the second top.

CHART 2-6

Inverted Head and Shoulders

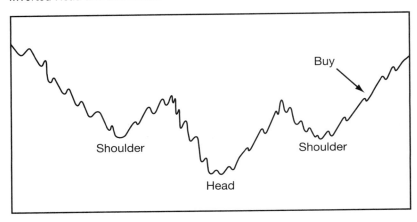

Refer to Chart 2-6. The inverted head and shoulders bottom-ing pattern is the upside-down image of the head and shoulders topping pattern. This bottoming pattern may develop at the end of a bear market. After the first shoulder and the head have formed, informed investors watch for the rise from the bottom of the second shoulder. Buying when the uptrend develops provides an opportu-nity for a large long-term capital gain.

Refer to Chart 2-7. The rounding bottom pattern is shaped like a saucer that converts a downtrend into an uptrend. During the accumulation period, knowledgeable investors realize the stock is selling at bargain prices and buy all the shares being offered. Grad-ually, the buying demand absorbs the supply of shares and an uptrend develops. The time to buy is when two or more short-term ascending bottoms appear in the chart.

Refer to Chart 2-8. The double bottom is a third bottoming pat-tern. Investors note the low prices at the first bottom. When the market index returns to that lowest level again, many buyers are eager to purchase those bargains. As the supply of available stock diminishes, the prices start to rise and form a new uptrend. The time to buy is when two or more short-term ascending bottoms appear in the move up from the second bottom.

CHART 2-7

Rounding Bottom

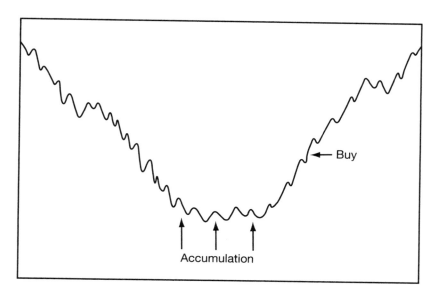

CHART 2-8

Double Bottom

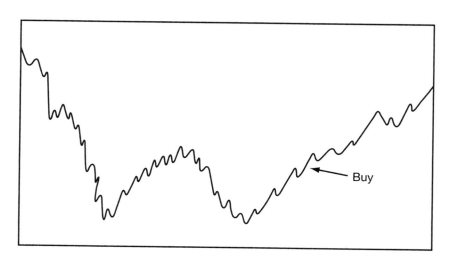

PATTERN VARIATIONS

The patterns you have just seen were drawn so as to be easy to recognize. There are many variations in the form of the patterns. Some of the different shapes you might see are: a head and shoulders pattern with more than one shoulder on either side of the head; a rounding bottom or top that may have jagged areas and bumps; double tops that may be at slightly different heights; double bottoms that may be at unequal depths and may extend into triple or quadruple bottoms. These and many other variations are what make chart interpretation an art. There will also be times when the economic data that affects stock prices has many conflicting trends, and there will be no discernable patterns.

CHARTS OF MARKET INDEXES

Now that you know what to look for, you can test your ability to identify the market phases and the topping and bottoming patterns in the charting services provided on the Internet. The index we will use as our proxy for the market is the Standard & Poor's 500 Index of stocks because it is the most representative of the thousands of stocks traded on the exchanges.

Here's how you can check the up-to-date price chart of the Standard & Poor's Composite Index on the Yahoo! Finance Web site. Enter finance.yahoo.com into your Internet search slot. At the Yahoo! Finance Web site, enter the symbol for the S&P 500 Index, (^GSPC). A screen giving information on the index appears. On the left-hand side of the screen click on the menu item "Technical Analysis." The screen that appears shows a selection of time ranges for the chart. Click on 5y (five years). This screen also shows a selection of moving averages. Click on EMA (exponential moving average) 200 (200 days). Now scroll down to see the chart you have requested. The blue line shows the five-year history of the S&P 500 Index. The red line is the 200-day exponential moving average. Here are the characteristics to look for to determine which phase the market is in.

In the bull market phase, the red line is slanting upward for at least three months. The blue line is making short-term tops and bottoms above the red line and shows no topping out pattern such as a rounding, double, or head and shoulders top.

If the market is in a range-bound phase, the red moving average proceeds in a horizontal direction. The blue line is also moving horizontally. It can be fluctuating just above, below, or criss-crossing the red line. These horizontal movements illustrate the lack of both upward and downward momentum in the market.

If the market is in a bear phase, the red line is slanting downward for at least three months. The blue line is also slanting downward and is making short-term tops and bottoms below the red line. The blue line does not show any bottoming out pattern such as a rounding bottom, double bottom, or inverted head and shoulders pattern.

Note: It may take several months before you see any of the patterns that have been illustrated in this chapter. But by checking the S&P Composite Index of 500 stocks periodically, you should eventually identify a pattern that indicates which phase the market is in or if it is making a top or a bottom.

ADAPTING TO MARKET PHASES

Each of the market phases has implications for investors. The bullish phase calls for an aggressive style in which investors buy investments with the objective of achieving capital gains. The range-bound phase calls for a balanced investment style in which investors make investments for both capital growth and income flow. The bearish phase calls for a conservative approach aimed at the preservation of capital through the ownership of bonds and other relatively safe investments.

The aggressive investing procedures and actions to make capital gains during a bull market will be described in Chapter 3. The activities appropriate for implementing a balanced style during a range-bound market will be described in Chapter 4. And the investment tactics intended to preserve capital will be presented in Chapter 5.

3

RIDING THE BULL

INTRODUCTION

The most exciting and rewarding time to be invested in stocks is during the bull market phase. Stock prices rise because of an improving economy and increasing company earnings. Interest rates are favorably low. Investors' enthusiasm grows as the market goes up month after month. The financial television show anchors and guests play the role of cheerleaders. The general mood in the investment community is one of great optimism based on an abundance of capital gains.

The key to profiting from this type of bouyant stock market is to get in early. As indicated in Chapter 2, the ideal time to get in is when you see a completed bottoming pattern. Fortunately, most bull markets last for several years. Once the uptrend has been established, the most rewarding investment style is to become more risk tolerant and aggressive to take advantage of the opportunities. This chapter presents procedures for finding stocks with good upside potential during a bull market.

INVESTING AGGRESSIVELY

In a bull market, the objective is to purchase stocks that can make large capital gains. To qualify for selection, the stock should have the following characteristics:

- The price of the stock is in an established uptrend showing two, three, or more sequential rising bottoms.
- The volume of trading in the stock is above its historical average.
- Its 200-day moving average is trailing the price upward and is ascending at an angle of 35 degrees or higher.

The combination of these factors indicate the stock price has strong upward momentum.

ANALYZING STOCK PRICE PATTERNS

One of the best sources of information on stocks that may meet these qualifications is on the Web site, www.clearstation.com. When you are ready to engage in some research, here is a procedure by which you can find profitable investments.

Go to the Web site. The A-list of the notable stocks for the day is shown in the center of the home page. Note the stock symbols in the following four categories.

1. "Record Price Break Out"
2. "Trending Up"
3. "Oversold"
4. "Analyst Upgrade"

Your primary focus should be on the stock symbols listed under the heading of "Trending Up." The price pattern with the most potential is one where the trend is just beginning. The second best category is "Record Price Break out." The third and forth categories are less likely to produce impressive capital gains. When you have time to check out a company represented by a stock symbol, follow this procedure.

Go to finance.yahoo.com and enter the stock symbol in the search slot. See the name of the company represented by that symbol. Write down the name and review the general information presented for that company. Then select "Technical Analysis" from the menu on the left side of the screen. From the list of time periods, one year has been preselected. From the row of moving averages, click on "200." Then press the lower scroll button to see the chart you have made. To help you evaluate the contents of this chart and the others you will make, some illustrations are presented on the following pages.

STOCK PRICES AND MOVING AVERAGES

Charts 3-1, 3-2, and 3-3 show price and moving average patterns that qualify stocks for purchase. As you look at these charts keep the following factors in mind to help in your evaluations:

- A moving average that follows a horizontal path is a no growth pattern.
- A moving average that rises at an angle of 5 degrees or less represents negligible growth.
- A moving average rising at 10 to 15 degrees is a slow growth situation.
- A moving average rising at 20 to 30 degrees is growing at a medium pace.
- A moving average rising at 35 to 45 degrees indicates growth at a fast pace.
- A moving average rising at an angle steeper than 45 degrees can produce a large capital gain in a short period of time, but has the risk of an equally fast decline.

Refer to Chart 3-1. This is an ideal relationship between the price and the moving average because the price stays well above the moving average. This type of wide gap between the moving average and the price of a stock is an indication of strong price momentum to the upside. This stock price is rising at an angle of 35 degrees, which indicates the stock is capable of a large gain in a short time period.

Refer to Chart 3-2. Here there is a changing relationship between the stock price and the moving average. The gap between

CHART 3-1

Ideal Stock Price and Moving Average Relationship

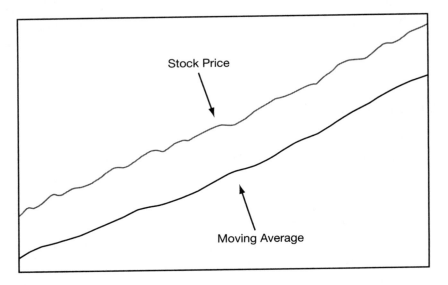

CHART 3-2

Acceptable Stock Price and Moving Average Relationship

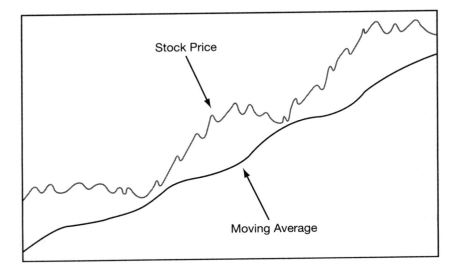

the price and the moving average fluctuates from wide to almost nothing. This indicates that demand for the stock is inconsistent. Investors' attitudes toward the stock vary widely from time to time, which causes the rise in price to be sporatic. However, as long as the stock price manages to stay above the average and the average keeps rising, the stock is acceptable as an investment. But the type of pattern shown in the Chart 3-1 is preferable.

Refer to Chart 3-3. This chart shows a stock price and its moving average rising at an angle of approximately 10 degrees. This slow rate of rise during a bull market is indicative of a minimal performance by the company. Investors have some doubts about the company's prospects. The periodic declines of the stock price toward the moving average are an indication of those uncertainties. This stock is minimally acceptable because of the low rate of rise and the lack of consistent demand for the investment. The stock and moving average patterns shown in Charts 3-1 and 3-2 are preferable because of the higher rate of ascent.

Refer to Chart 3-4. Here the stock and its moving average are in downtrends. When a moving average follows a stock price down, it indicates a strong conviction on the part of investors that

CHART 3-3

Minimally Acceptable Stock and Moving Average Relationship

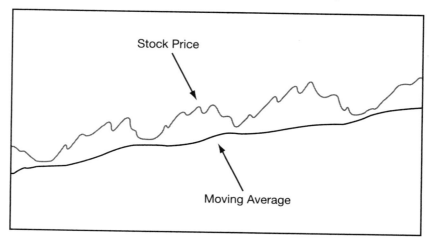

CHART 3-4

CHART 3-4

Unqualified by Falling Price

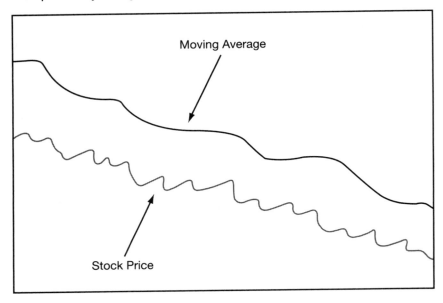

the prospects for the company are negative. Until the company takes aggressive action to improve its operating results and produce increasing earnings, the price of the stock is likely to continue declining. A pattern like this during any market phase is a warning sign against making a purchase.

Refer to Chart 3-5. This stock price is fluctuating above and below the moving average, which is going in a horizontal direction. This pattern implies investors' ambivilance about the prospects for the company. The high-risk aspect of this stock price and moving average relationship is that on one of the downward penetrations the price keeps dropping and a downtrend develops. This stock is unqualified for purchase based on its lack of upward momentum and the high risk of a capital loss.

Refer to Chart 3-6. Here a stock price and its moving average are rising at a rate of approximately five degrees. The gap between the price and its moving average is very narrow, indicating that the level of investor confidence is low. The rate of return from this

CHART 3-5

Unqualified by Flat Price

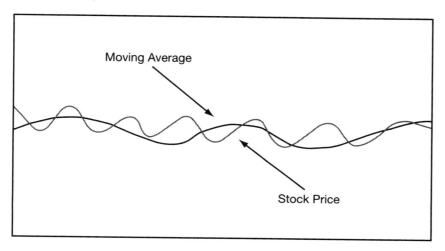

CHART 3-6

Unqualified by Low Angle of Ascent

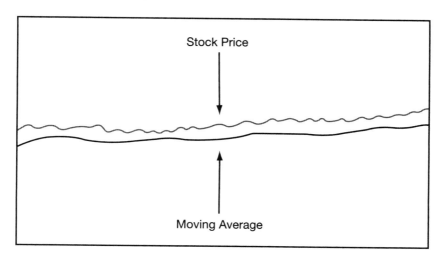

investment is minimal after inflation and other costs are subtracted from any gains. This stock is not qualified for purchase because of the low angle of rise and the narrow gap.

Refer to Chart 3-7. This chart shows a rare price pattern involving potential high reward and risk. In this case, it is crucial to get on board early or not at all because there is no way to predict at what level this stock price will start into a free fall. It is certain that at some point there will be no more buyers willing to speculate on further advances in price, and it will then probably decline as fast as it rose. If you have a stock that participates in this type of parabolic rise, you can protect your profit by using a trailing stop loss order. This order should be raised after each new high in the stock price, and it should be placed just below where the most recent short-term price decline stopped. When the stock price starts dropping fast, your stop loss order would be executed at the market, and with good luck you will still have most of your profit.

CHART 3-7

Riding a Parabolic Price Curve

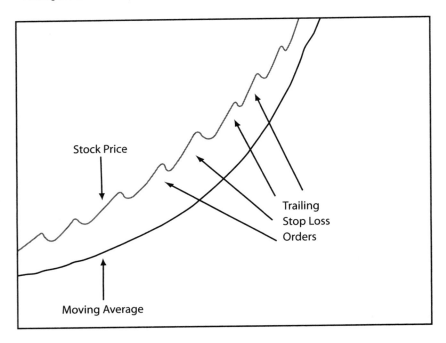

Here is a review of the important features of the relationships among stock prices and their moving averages.

Desirable Features

- The stock price leads the moving average higher.
- There is a gap between the stock price and the moving average.
- Wide, consistent gaps are better than narrow or fluctuating gaps.
- The moving average rises at an angle of more than 20 degrees.

Undesirable Features

- The stock price drops steadily and the moving average follows.
- The stock price fluctuates above and below the moving average.
- The moving average rises at an angle of less than 5 degrees.
- The moving average proceeds in a horizontal direction.

Note: If none of the stock price charts show a desirable relationship between the price and the moving average, the ClearStation home page provides a new set of stock symbols every business day.

FUNDAMENTAL ANALYSIS

In addition to distinguishing between a qualified and an unqualified stock from a technical point of view, it is helpful to look at the company itself from the fundamental point of view. This includes a review of the company's financial performance data. The following section describes some of the information about a company to help you decide if it is qualified from a fundamental perspective.

At the Yahoo! Finance home page, finance.yahoo.com, enter a stock symbol in "Get Quotes" and click "Go," then look at the menu on the left and click on "Key Statistics." When this screen comes up, find the heading "Valuation Measures" and look at the item "Forward P/E" (price-to-earnings ratio). If the company's stock is priced reasonably, this figure will be about 16 or 17, plus or minus several points. If it is much higher, the stock is overpriced unless the company's earnings are increasing at a very fast pace.

Under the heading "Profitability," the "Profit Margin" and the "Operating Margin" should both be positive, and the higher the better. Under the heading "Income Statement," the "Quarterly Revenue Growth" should be 10 percent or more. Under the heading of "Cash Flow Statement," the item "Free Cash Flow" should be a positive number—the higher the better.

The technical and fundamental evaluation procedures should be repeated for each stock of interest to you. They provide an objective basis for making purchase decisions. Subjecting A-list stocks to this type of examination should enable you to come up with a selection of stocks that will allow you to ride a bull market to large capital gains.

ASSESSING RISK

Selecting individual stocks for capital gains is appropriate during bull markets so long as you are aware of the risk involved with each selection. In this section, you will see an Internet source where you can check on the risk level for any stock.

When you are ready to start this activity, go to Web address www.moneycentral.msn.com. At the home page, click on "Investing." Then click on "Stocks." Under "Research Tools" click on "StockScouter." Enter the symbol of a stock in the "Name or Symbol" slot and click on "Go." The resulting display presents a number from 1, which is the worst rating, to 10, which is the best rating, on the prospects for the company. To the right there are scales showing a risk versus return comparison. It is very desirable that the return bar be longer than the risk bar. Assess this relationship to make sure it is acceptable in terms of your tolerance for risk.

4

A BALANCING ACT

INTRODUCTION

There are times when the upward progress of a bull market stalls.
Market analysts say the market is consolidating its gains. These
resting periods can be as short as 6 months or as long as 15 years
(1965 to 1980). During these periods, the market fluctuates below
the new ceiling and is referred to as being *range-bound*. The top of
the range is determined by an area of resistance. A support level
establishes the bottom of the range. This chapter provides guidance
on how to manage your portfolio when the market is range-bound.

ADJUSTING YOUR PORTFOLIO

Although the upward momentum of the total market is blocked,
there may be a few individual stocks that maintain their uptrends.
You should evaluate each stock in your portfolio to identify those
whose upward progress has not been stopped and hold them for
further capital gains. Stocks that display negative price and moving
average patterns should be sold. To review those patterns see
Charts 3-4, 3-5, and 3-6.

During a range-bound market, a worthwhile research activity
is to find investments that can provide a steady flow of income.

This is important because the length of time the market will remain range-bound is unpredictable. Since capital gains are limited during this period, adding a high-income flow builds up the assets in your portfolio and provides the capital to make new purchases or for other purposes. The next two sections of this chapter outline procedures for finding closed-end funds and real estate investment trusts that can produce high-income flow.

CLOSED-END FUNDS

One of the best places to search for high income is in closed-end funds. Each of these funds issues a limited number of shares. The shares in these funds trade like stocks, so they can be bought and sold when the market is open, and their price charts can be analyzed the same way that the price charts of individual stocks are evaluated.

The managers of closed-end funds invest in a wide variety of assets, including common and preferred stocks, U.S. government bonds, foreign bonds, domestic and foreign corporate bonds, and municipal bonds. Because of this diversification, these funds have lower risk than many individual stocks and nondiversified open-ended mutual funds. The statement of objectives for closed-end funds specifies that income generation is their primary goal, and this objective is achieved through active management strategies.

Barron's weekly magazine lists these funds in the Market Week section under the heading of "Closed-End Funds." There are two main classes of funds—those that invest in stocks and those that invest in bonds and other debt instruments. The level of yield from the stock funds is the combination of dividends and any capital gain or loss. The level of yield from the bond funds is the amount of income distributions as a percentage of market price. This data allows you to compare the return among the individual funds.

Also listed is each fund's net asset value (NAV). This is the total value of the assets in the fund's portfolio minus the total amount of the fund's liabilities, divided by the number of shares outstanding. The current price quotes are compared against the net asset value to see whether each fund is selling at a discount or a premium.

Purchasing a closed-end fund that has a high yield at a discount provides a high-income flow and the possibility of a capital gain.

Researching Closed-End Funds

The Association of Closed-End Funds maintains a Web site that provides a large quantity of helpful information. When you are ready to research these funds, the starting point is at Web address www.cefa.com. At this home page you will see a variety of educational information that provides a comprehensive description of closed-end funds.

At the right-hand side of the screen, note the title "Today's Leaders." Under that title, click on "Discount" and a list of the 25 most heavily discounted funds appears. Select several funds and write down their symbols. Each of the symbols you select can be entered into the search slot in the top left corner of the page. For each symbol entered, information on the fund appears, including net asset value, current market price, percentage of discount, and return on investment. More details can be obtained where it says "Click Here for More Information."

Repeat this procedure for each fund you have selected and note which funds are most in line with your objectives. Then return to the home page. At the right-hand side of the screen, note the heading, "S&P Stock Reports." Click on that, and a list of 12 funds with no regard for discount or premium pricing is presented. Select several funds, note their symbols, return to the home page, insert each symbol into the search slot, and click "GO." The basic information on each fund is shown, and more details are available at "Click Here for More Information." If you want it, a two-page printout of the additional details can be made. By printing those documents, you will have a set of reference materials on the group of funds that reflects your interests.

Lists of Closed-End Funds

Barron's magazine divides closed-end funds into 14 categories. Four of these are more likely to provide high-income flow. Here are their titles:

Specialized Equity Funds

World Equity Funds

Investment Grade Bond Funds

World Income Funds

All these funds invest on an international basis. This provides the fund managers the freedom to invest wherever there are good prospects and to take advantage of opportunities for capital gains not generally available in a range-bound domestic market.

After selecting fund names and symbols from these lists, return to the home page of the Association of Closed-End Funds (www.cefa.com) to get the details.

REAL ESTATE INVESTMENT TRUSTS

Real estate investment trusts (REITs) are required to pay out at least 90 percent of their earnings to their shareholders. This makes them very attractive to investors seeking high income. There are two main types of real estate investment trusts:

1. Those that invest in real properties and whose earnings are based primarily on income from rentals

2. Those that invest in mortgage-backed securities

Both types can be profitable, but the earnings of those dealing in mortgages are volatile because changes in the relationship between short- and long-term interest rates can have a major effect on their profit margins.

Some of the real estate investment trusts that own real properties write leases that run for 10 years, which makes their rental income flow very reliable. They may own health care facilities, regional malls, neighborhood shopping centers, office buildings, apartment complexes, industrial parks, self-storage facilities, amusement parks, assisted-living communities, and other types of income-producing properties.

Real estate investment trust funds are also available. These funds own more than one type of real estate investment trust and often more than 50 different individual properties. This diversification results in a lower level of risk than owning just one type of property. Like individual real estate investment trusts, these funds are required to pay at least 90 percent of their earnings to their stockholders. A good time to buy a real estate investment trust or fund is when long-term interest rates are high.

To research real estate investment trust funds and individual trusts, go to the National Association of Real Estate Investment Trusts Web site at www.investinREITS.com. Click on "Closed-End Funds." A list of funds and their stock market symbols is presented. Make a note of several funds and their symbols. Then select a symbol and click on it. The Yahoo! Finance page for that fund appears and provides basic information on the fund you selected. The most important items to check are the dollar amount of the dividend for the year and the percentage of yield to make sure they are high enough to satisfy your need for income.

At the left side of the screen, click on "Technical Analysis." When the choices are presented, select "200" from the row of moving averages and select "RSI." (Relative Strength Index) from the row of indicators. A time period of one year has been preselected, but you can increase or decrease the amount of time covered by the chart if you desire. Press the lower right scroll button to see the chart you have made. You can then analyze the chart by looking for the positive features that qualify it for your portfolio. Repeat this procedure for several of the other fund symbols and compare the results. After you complete this process, decide if you want to include any of these funds in your portfolio to provide income flow during the range-bound market.

To do a comparison study of individual real estate investment trust stocks, go back to the National Association of Real Estate Investment Trusts Web site homepage (www.investinREITs.com) and click on "REITs by Ticker Symbol." A list of stocks is presented so you can compare the stocks as you did the funds. You will then be able to make the decision as to whether to buy individual stocks or funds, or both.

TRADING FOR CAPITAL GAINS

With a buy and hold strategy, getting capital gains in a range-bound market is difficult. An alternative approach for making capital gains in this type of market is buying and selling within a vertical trading range formed by some individual stock price patterns. Chart 4-1 illustrates this technique.

Purchases should be made near the support level and sales should be made near the resistance level. If the overall market stays range-bound for an extended period, you should be able to find several individual stocks that develop this price pattern, thus providing some opportunities for trading actively for capital gains.

To find candidates for this type of trading, check the list of most actively traded stocks in your daily newspaper. To find the symbols for these stocks, go to Web site finance.yahoo.com, click on "Symbol Lookup," and enter the name of the company in the search slot. Then click on the stock symbol for the company and look for trading range patterns after clicking on "Technical Analysis" from the menu on the left and making charts of at least a year in duration.

CHART 4-1

Making Capital Gains in a Trading Range

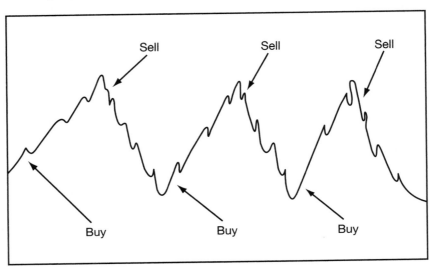

Here are some points to remember for getting the most from trading stocks this way while staying within your level of risk tolerance. Use only a small percentage of your assets. If you have never traded like this before, start with very small purchases. As you develop skill in this technique, increase the size of your purchases. Use an Internet broker that charges very low commissions to keep your costs low. Look for trading ranges with wide vertical distances to increase your potential profits for each round trip transaction.

CHAPTER

5

DEFEATING THE BEAR

INTRODUCTION

After some investors have made large capital gains, they become overconfident during a bull market run up. They may become convinced their stocks can only keep going higher. But nothing lasts forever, and the stock market periodically enters a bearish phase when prices decline swiftly to much lower levels. Being successful in the market not only involves making large capital gains, but, just as important, keeping what has been won. This chapter is intended to prevent you from being surprised by the arrival of a bear market and to help you readjust your portfolio to preserve your assets.

The three activities you should engage in to defend against the damage a bear market can cause are:

1. Recognizing the conditions that set the stage
2. Spotting the top of a bull market as it develops
3. Switching portfolio contents to the types of investments that will preserve your gains

Each of these activities will be explained in the following sections.

RECOGNIZING A TOP

Market tops are characterized by excessive speculation and enthusiasm on the part of active investors. Having watched stocks rise
consistently in recent years, many market participants become convinced the market is a one way street to riches. At parties and other
social gatherings, they proudly share stories about their profitable
trades. The media presents a united chorus of approval for buying
stocks based on upward momentum. Anchors of financial shows
on television become cheerleaders and deliver enthusiastic reports
on each advance to new highs. Everybody wants a piece of the
action and the consensus opinion is that the market will continue
its upward run. These are the social signs the stage is being set for
the end of the bull market run. To confirm these signs that speculation has become excessive, prudent investors look for additional
indicators that the bull market is entering its final stage.

TECHNICAL INDICATORS

The top of a bull market can be seen in both the chart of the
Standard & Poor's 500 Index of stocks and in the charts of individ-
ual stocks. These topping-out patterns were shown in Chapter 2.
(See Charts 2-3, 2-4, and 2-5.)

Another technical indication of the end of a bull market is the
relationship of the Standard & Poor's 500 Index of stocks to the 200-
day moving average of the index. After a bull market has been in
existence for several years, the potential end can be predicted in the
following manner. Go to the home page of the Yahoo! Finance Web
site at finance.yahoo.com and enter the symbol for the Standard &
Poor's 500 Index of stocks (^GSPC) in the search slot. Click "GO"
and the data on the index appears. Then select "Technical Analysis"
from the menu on the left side of the screen. From the selection of
parameters that appears, select "5y" (5 years) and "200." Then
scroll down to see the chart. The blue line is the value of the index.
The red line is the 200-day moving average. Check this relationship
at least once a week. When the value of the index drops through the
moving average, it is a technical sign the bull market has ended.

ECONOMIC SIGNS

There are also economic warning signs of the end of a bull market. When interest rates rise they create a downward pressure on the earnings of companies that borrow money to run or expand their businesses. The rising cost of money strains the finances of these companies and reduces their profits. This creates a drag on the national economy.

The most knowledgeable and sophisticated investors stay aware of these factors that precede a recession, and they start selling months in advance of the actual decline. Their early selling helps to precipitate the bearish phase of the stock market.

SIGNALS FROM COMMODITIES

Another sign of an approaching bear market is a decline in commodity prices. Much of the demand for commodities is tied in directly with a strong economy. As the condition of the economy begins to weaken, there is less demand for many commodities and price downtrends begin to appear. A decline in commodity prices is one of the early warning signs of a developing problem in the economy. The Commodity Research Bureau (CRB) Index is published at www.crbtrader.com. By checking this Web site periodically, you can be alerted to an impending bear market.

CYCLICAL INDUSTRIES DECLINE FIRST

Another warning of an imminent bear market is a price decline in the stocks of cyclical companies such as manufacturers of durable goods, airlines, hotels, casinos, construction firms, and restaurant chains. Companies in these businesses are more sensitive to an impending decline in the economy, and a fall in their stock prices serves as early evidence that a bear market is developing.

PRESERVING YOUR CAPITAL

The primary objective for investors during a bear market is the preservation of capital. This requires switching some assets in your portfolio into conservative investments such as bonds, money market accounts, and preferred stocks that pay high dividends. Listed below are some suggestions for investments appropriate for a bear market.

Zero Coupon Bonds

United States zero coupon bonds are among the safest investments because they are backed by the full faith and credit of the government. They sell at a discount and the purchaser receives full face value when the bond matures. The bondholder receives no interest during the holding period but has a capital gain at the completion of the transaction.

A comprehensive listing of U.S. zero coupon bonds is published every week in *Barron's* magazine in the Market Week section. These listings show the month and year of maturity, the bid and asked prices, the change in price for the week, and the percentage of yield.

These bonds can be purchased for any time period from a few months to 25 years. Bear markets may be as short as two years or less and as long as five years or more. Purchasing bonds that mature in about two years would provide a safe haven during a short bear market. If the decline lasts longer, after the bonds mature you can renew your position by buying bonds with a one-year maturity date to ride out the added time safely. Instead of losing capital, you will have a gain. Zero coupon bonds can be purchased from the Treasury Department at www.treasurydirect.gov, through a full-service stock and bond brokerage company, or from the special services department of an Internet broker. They are available in units with a face value of $1,000 each.

Municipal Bonds

Municipal bonds are issued by states, counties, cities, and other public entities for construction projects or other purposes. The safest type is a general obligation bond issued by a state. The term *general obligation* means the resources of the entire state provide financial support for the bond issue, and the bond will be redeemed by the state treasury when it matures or is called. Bonds not issued in the general obligation status should only be purchased if they are insured. By purchasing only general obligation and insured municipal bonds, you assure the relative safety of the investments.

Municipal bonds do not trade like stocks with changing price quotes throughout the day. Instead you must contact your broker and discuss the characteristics of the type of bond you want to buy and the interest rate you hope to receive. After the broker identifies a bond issue that meets your requirements, you tell the broker how many $1,000 bonds you want to purchase. The broker then makes inquiries to determine if those bonds are available in the quantity you want. If they are, the broker gives you the offering price of the seller. If the price is acceptable, you authorize the broker to make the purchase on your behalf.

If interest rates are high, you may be able to purchase a bond at a discount from par value, which means you have a capital gain when the bond matures or is called. Spread your purchases to mature over a two-to-five year period so you can cash in your investments after the bear market has ended.

Preferred Stocks

The name of this type of stock refers to its preferred status to the common stock in reference to dividend payments. This requires the dividend on the preferred issue to be paid before any dividend can be paid on the common stock. Many preferred stocks are issued at a par value of $25 and usually have a call date five years from the date of issue. On the call date, the company refunds the par value to the holder if the stock is called. Some preferred issues have no stated maturity date and those issues continue paying the quarterly dividends until they are redeemed.

An excellent source of information on preferred stocks is the Web site www.QuantumOnLine.com. Enter the symbol of a stock in the search slot and this site provides a general description of the preferred issue along with a price chart, the credit rating of the issue, the annual dividend amount, the percent yield, the ex-dividend dates, and the dates dividends are paid. Dividends paid by preferred stocks are often higher than dividends paid by the common stocks.

When buying a preferred stock, look for one available at par value or at a discount that has an AAA, AA, or A rating by Standard & Poor's rating service. Avoid paying any premium over par value as you would have a loss when the issue is called. Try to find one whose call date is at least four years ahead of the current date so you can get your money back after most or all of the decline of the bear market has occurred.

Money Market Funds

In a bear market, holding some cash is prudent because panic selling in some stocks provides rare opportunities for purchasing stocks at distressed prices. As a bear market approaches the bottom, you will probably see some stocks make all-time lows on huge trading volumes and then recover to close with a gain for the day. Market technicians designate this event as a key reversal day and it signifies that many stockholders have capitulated and sold at the bottom. At this point, experienced investors are convinced prices are very likely to rise a considerable distance and they start buying stocks. If you have been holding some cash through the market decline, you will be in a position to buy one or more stocks for potentially large capital gains.

It is a good tactic to hold some cash because, as the market declines, the purchasing power of cash increases. Cash held through a declining market can buy more shares at each lower level. And the dollar reaches its maximum relative purchasing power at the end of the bear market.

SUGGESTED PORTFOLIO CONTENT

Since U.S. government zero coupon bonds are the safest investment, they should be the largest portion of a bear market portfolio. Municipal bonds are almost as safe as U.S. bonds when they are issued by state governments as a general obligation on the resources of the state. Preferred stocks bought at par value or at a discount can deliver high dividends to increase the income from a portfolio. And a cash component provides the ability to take advantage of rare bargains at the bottom of the long decline. In view of these characteristics, the following portfolio mix is suggested for your review. It can be adjusted to fit with your financial objective and needs and your level of risk tolerance.

Portfolio Mix

U.S. government bonds	40%
General obligation municipal bonds issued by states	30%
Preferred stocks rated AAA, AA, or A	20%
Cash in a money market fund	10%
Total:	100%

6

PICKING WINNERS IN THE STOCK MARKET

INTRODUCTION

There are people who use the stock market as a place for speculating and there are those who take a conservative approach. For these two very different groups and for investors with moderate styles, picking winners is a very satisfying part of investing in the market. Some investors want stocks that rise fast in a short time. Others are looking for stocks that can provide gains over a longer time period. And investors wanting income flow prefer stocks that pay high dividends. If you relate to any of these goals, this chapter presents lists of stocks that have been screened to help you find what you are looking for.

The first list (see Table 6-1) contains stocks that have the potential of rising 35 percent in the short-term time period of up to six months. The second list (see Table 6-2) presents stocks that have the ability to sustain upward momentum over the intermediate term of 6 months to 1 year. These stocks also pay some dividends. The third list (see Tables 6-3 through 6-6) is for those investors who want reliable high-income flow and a chance for some capital gains. Select the list that reflects your interest, follow the guidelines for evaluating the investments, and you should be able to find one or more that are appropriate for you. However, remember there is some risk in every investment and if you buy a stock at the wrong time, it will be lower in value at some point.

PICKING SHORT-TERM WINNERS

To assist you in finding stocks that have the potential for quick appreciation, review Table 6-1. These are small, relatively unpublicized companies chosen because their stocks have demonstrated the ability to make large gains in a short period of time. To check on the probability for each stock to make future gains, go to www.finance. yahoo.com. Enter a stock symbol in the search slot and click "GO." From the menu that appears on the left of the screen, select "Technical Analysis." From the next screen select "50" from the row titled "Moving Averages." (Using this short-term moving average will help you determine when to sell.) Then scroll down to see the chart

TABLE 6-1

Short-Term Winners

Company Name	Company Symbol	Type of Business
Akamai Technologies	AKAM	Provides problem-solving services and software for businesses.
Allegheny Energy	AYE	Provides electricity and natural gas to rural and surburban areas.
Applix	APLX	Sells information technology to help companies automate, analyze, and improve operations.
Art Technology	ARTG	Helps businesses market their brands more effectively.
Citrix Systems	CTXS	Sells access infrastructure software services in the Americas, Asia, Europe, and the Middle East.
Comtech Group	COGO	Designs and sells modules for mobile handsets and telecom equipment.
Dril-Quip	DRQ	Sells off shore drilling equipment for oil and gas wells.
Eltek	ELTK	Sells printed circuit boards to aerospace, medical, and electronics industries in Europe and Israel.
Exploration Company of Delaware	TXCO	Explores for and develops oil and gas properties.

Company Name	Company Symbol	Type of Business
First Cash Financial	FCFS	Owns and operates chains of pawn shops and Advance Pay Day stores.
Fargo Electronics	FRGO	Sells secure systems for making identity cards for drivers, the military, social services and professions.
Guess?	GES	Sells casual apparel and accessories for men, women, and children.
Infosonics	IFO	Sells wireless handsets and other communications devices.
Kirby	KEX	Provides marine transportation and diesel engine services to barges and oil companies.
Ladish	LDSH	Provides forged and cast metal parts for jet engines and industries worldwide.
Logitech International	LOGI	Sells Webcams, speakers, consoles, and cordless mice for computers.
Middleby	MIDD	Sells food preparation equipment to institutions.
Mobile Mini	MINI	Provides storage containers, office units, and custom built structures for companies.
Mossimo	MOSS	Sells men's, women's, and children's apparel, jewelry, handbags, and watches.
Oakley	OO	Sells specialty eyewear and sports clothing.
RSA Security	RSAS	Provides online security for business and protects consumer identities.
Smithway Motor Express	SMXC	Provides flatbed transportation to shippers, steel, and construction industries.
TETRA Technologies	TTI	Provides services, supplies, and decommissioning for oil rigs.
TradeStation Group	TRAD	Provides trading platform and services for active traders.
Transocean	RIG	Provides off shore drilling services for oil and gas wells.
TTM Technologies	TTM	Sells multilayer circuit boards for networking, infrastructure, and medical markets.
VAALCO Energy	EGY	Produces oil and natural gas and has reserves of 8 million barrels of oil and 54 million cubic feet of natural gas.
Veritas DGC	VTS	Provides geophysical data for oil and gas companies.
WPCS International	WPCS	Provides engineering services for wireless communication systems.

Note: To improve your chances of finding winners, it would be best to wait for a bull or range-bound market. If you try to find short- or intermediate-term winners in a bear market, positive results will be very difficult to achieve. Instead, follow the investing guidelines for bear markets in Chapter 5.

you have made and check the price in blue and the moving average in red for the following qualifying features:

1. The price is above the moving average and there is a continuing gap of space between them.
2. The moving average is rising at a rate of 35 degrees or more.
3. The gap has lasted for two months or longer.

Stocks that have these features are more likely to achieve large gains within 6 months than those that do not. Refer to Charts 6-1 and 6-2. These charts illustrate two desirable relationships between stock prices and their moving averages. Then refer to Chart 6-3, which shows when a positive relationship between price and moving average has ended. When the price falls through the moving average, the upside momentum has been lost and the stock should be sold.

Note that after calling up the first technical analysis chart display you can get a technical display for each additional stock by entering its symbol in the slot labeled "Get Technical Analysis Chart for."

CHART 6-1

Stock Price Moves Up through Moving Average

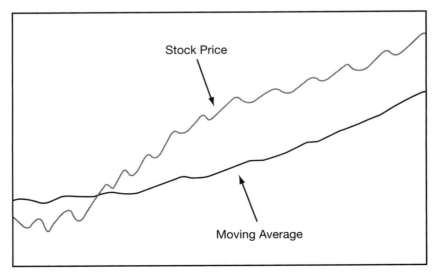

CHART 6-2

Stock Price Stays above Moving Average

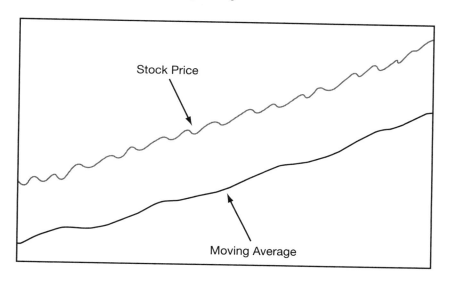

CHART 6-3

Stock Price Falls through Moving Average

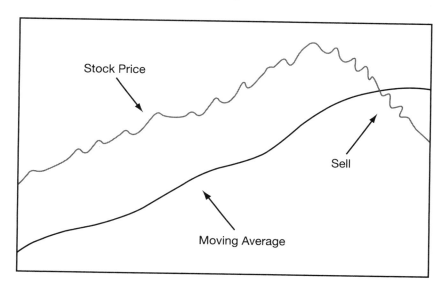

PICKING INTERMEDIATE-TERM WINNERS

The companies listed in Table 6-2 have been selected because there is consistent demand for their products and/or services. They also have price-to-earnings ratios that are reasonable in relation to their rate of earnings growth. And they pay dividends and have the potential for large capital gains in the intermediate term.

In the stock market, buying at the right time is the critical element in successful stock picking. To improve your chances of good timing, check each company's stock price pattern as shown in the "Technical Analysis" menu item provided by the Yahoo! Finance Web site at finance.yahoo.com. These charts show the current relationship between the stock price and the moving average. Compare the price patterns available from the Web site to the ones in Charts 6-1 and 6-2. This can be done by following the directions given in the preceding section and selecting the 100-day moving average that is comensurate with an intermediate time span. Look for price

TABLE 6-2

Intermediate-Term Potential Winners

Company Name and Type of Business	Company Symbol	P/E	Dividend Percentage
Allegheny Technology High performance metals	ATI	16	0.5
Allied Capital Makes loans to businesses	ALD	7	8.0
Bank of South Carolina Commercial banking	BKSC	23	3.3
Canon Copy machines & cameras	CAJ	17	1.2
Cascade Bancorp Commercial and retail banking	CACB	23	1.4
Crane Electronic systems for airlines	CR	17	1.3
Credit Suisse Group Investment banking	CSR	14	4.1

Company Name and Type of Business	Company Symbol	P/E	Dividend Percentage
Cummins Heavy duty engines	CMI	11	1.1
FedEx Package & document delivery	FDX	20	0.3
Freeport McMoran B Mining gold, silver, and copper	FCX	15	2.3
Frontier Oil Refines crude oil	FTO	11	0.2
Harsco Provides construction equipment and services	HSC	22	1.6
Hewlett-Packard Computers and related equipment	HPQ	35	1.0
J & J Snack Foods Snack foods and beverages	JJSF	24	0.9
JPMorgan Chase Investment banking	JPM	18	3.2
Kimco Realty Shopping centers (REIT)	KIM	24	3.4
Lufkin Industries Oil industry products and services	LUFK	18	0.8
Manor Care Skilled nursing services and therapy	HCR	27	1.3
Meridian Bioscience Disease diagnosis kits	VIVO	41	2.0
Nokia ADS Wireless communication devices	NOK	18	1.8
Northern Trust Investment banking	NTRS	20	1.7
Ormat Technologies Geothermal power plants	ORA	67	0.3
Principal Financial Group Financial services for retirement	PFG	16	1.2

Note: Price-to-earnings ratios and dividend percentages are as of the date of publication and are subject to change. To get current information, check Web site finance.yahoo.com.

patterns and moving average relationships that have the following characteristics:

1. The stock price is above the moving average and there is a gap between them. (The wider the gap is, the better are the prospects for a large gain.)
2. The gap should be at least 4 months in length.
3. The moving average is rising at an angle of at least 20 degrees.

CHECKING RISK VERSUS RETURN

To help you make your purchase decisions, the factor of risk versus return should be evaluated. To do this go to www.moneycentral .msn.com. At this home page click on "Investing." On the screen that comes up, click on "Stocks" in the lower menu bar. In the next screen find the heading "Research Tools" and click on "StockScouter." Enter the stock symbol in this search slot and click "Go." This brings up "StockScouter Rating" and this number should be six or higher. Next, look to the right where "Expected Risk/Return" is shown. The risk bar should be shorter than the return bar. This relationship indicates the risk to return comparison is favorable for investing. Repeat this procedure for each stock symbol. Then compare the results for the various stocks and rank them for the lowest risks and the highest returns. This ranking provides guidance for sequencing your purchases.

INVESTING FOR INCOME

As an alternative to picking stocks for capital gains and waiting for the profits to materialize, some investors prefer to invest for high-income flow to be obtained quickly. Holding investments that pay high dividends or interest is especially appropriate in a range-bound market when stocks that make large capital gains are harder to find. Below are some categories of investments and individual equities that provide these high returns.

Huge deposits of oil, oil sands, and natural gas exist in Canada. As long as the price of oil and natural gas remain high, there will be strong incentives for companies to develop these deposits. Much of the development of these resources is financed by royalty trusts. These trusts pay out most of their income in the form of dividend disbursements. Some of these trusts pay 10 percent or more. With the reserves of crude oil and natural gas being depleted around the globe, the huge resources in Canada will be a reliable source for these commodities in the coming years. Table 6-3 presents a sampling of these trusts.

Real estate investment trusts are required to pay out 90 percent of their earnings, and some of them do this on a monthly basis. They get much of their revenue from leasing rental properties. Some of the leases run for 10 years, which provides for a very reliable flow of income. Table 6-4 presents a sampling of REITs paying high dividends.

The stated objective of many tax-exempt bond funds is to invest their assets in bonds exempt from federal and state taxes. They buy a wide variety of bonds with a range of maturities to provide the advantage of diversification. They usually hold 50 or more individual

TABLE 6-3

Oil and Gas Royalty Trusts

Name of Trust	Symbol	Approximate Dividend Rate
Pengrowth Energy Trust	PGH	11%
Petrofund Energy Trust	PTF	9%
Prime West Energy Trust	PWI	12%
Provident Energy Trust	PVX	10%

Note: For a complete up-to-date listing of similar trusts, contact Newsletters Plus at 411 Palmer Avenue, Aptos, CA 95003; telephone: 1-800-276-7721.

TABLE 6-4

Real Estate Investment Trusts

Name of REIT	Symbol	Approximate Dividend Rate
Affordable Residences	ARC	7%
Thornburg Mortgage	TMA	10%
Glimcher Realty Trust	GRT	7%

Note: A complete up-to-date list of REITs is available at Web site www.investinREITS.com. To get information on a specific REIT, click on "REITs by Ticker Symbol."

bond issues in their portfolios to keep to reduce the impact of defaults. Depending on your tax bracket, your net income from this type of investment can be a couple of percentage points higher than the alternative of paying taxes. Table 6-5 presents a sampling of these tax-exempt bond funds.

High-yield bond funds invest in bonds that have low credit ratings by Standard & Poor's and other bond rating services. Investors who purchase these funds should be aware of the higher default risks associated with these funds compared to other funds that hold only highly rated bonds. Invest in these high-yield funds only if you have a high tolerance for risk and if your financial resources and other income are adequate to support your life style no matter how these funds perform. Table 6-6 presents a sampling of these funds.

TABLE 6-5

Tax-Exempt Bond Funds

Name of Bond Fund	Symbol	Approximate Interest Rate
Colonial High Income	CXE	6%
Eaton Vance Municipal Trust	EVN	6%
Municipal Holdings Fund	MHD	6%
Pioneer High Income	MAV	6%

Note: For an up-to-date complete listing of these funds, check the Closed-End Funds section of *Barron's* magazine.

TABLE 6-6

High-Yield Bond Funds

Name of Bond Fund	Symbol	Approximate Dividend Rate
Black Rock High Income	HIS	9%
Credit Suisse High Yield	DHY	10%
Dreyfus High Yield	DHF	9%
PIMCO High Income	PHK	9%
Salomon High Income II	HIX	8%

Note: For a complete up-to-date list of high-yield bond funds, check the Closed-End Funds section of *Barron's* magazine.

REVIEW AND PREVIEW

This chapter has provided investments of interest to three types of investors: those looking for short-term trades, those seeking intermediate-term trading opportunities, and those who want high income flow. In Chapter 9, investors who prefer a buy and hold strategy will have the opportunity to select a diversified portfolio of 10 companies that can be held for long-term capital gains.

7

GOLDEN OPPORTUNITIES

INTRODUCTION

The allure of gold dates from ancient times, when the Egyptian pharoahs wanted their facial likenesses preserved forever in the glorious shine of the metal that is impervious to corrosion. For more than 2000 years it has played a central role as a tangible storehouse of value. The unique characteristics of gold make it the favorite medium for the creation of fine jewelry and for some industrial uses. Aside from the ornamental and practical uses of gold, why might an investor want to own this precious metal?

Some conservative investors believe that owning gold is like having the protection of an insurance policy against negative financial trends or a catastrophe such as a nuclear, biological, or chemical attack on a major city by a terrorist group. Another potential disaster is a successful attack on a major Middle Eastern oil installation, which would result in skyrocketing oil prices. Some negative trends that could lead to serious financial problems are the growing national debt and the annual deficits in the national budget and in the balance of trade with other countries. At some point, these imbalances could have serious consequences like drastic declines in the value of the dollar or a major downward impact on the economy. If either of these negative conditions were to develop, gold and gold related investments could have dramatic increases in value.

GOLD BULLION

Gold bullion is produced by refining gold ore into bars. The price is fixed twice a day at the London Bullion Market Association. The fixed price is based on the amount of buy and sell orders at the time. The price does not stay fixed. The bid and asked quotes are soon changed as orders come in from commercial gold traders. At the Web site www.kitco.com, you can get charts showing the spot price of gold when the markets are open in London, New York, Sydney, and Hong Kong.

Gold can be bought for immediate delivery at the spot price, or for delivery at the end of the current month, or for forward months in the current or later years. This delayed delivery system is the basis for trading gold futures in the commodities markets. By checking to see whether the prices are rising or falling in the forward months, you can get a general idea of the direction of prices in the long term. However, the price for each forward month is subject to change day by day and there is a high degree of uncertainty as to where each future month's price will be when that month becomes the current month.

EXCHANGE-TRADED GOLD FUNDS

It is impractical for most investors to buy gold bullion because of the expenses of insuring, transporting, and storing it in a safe place. Exchange-traded gold funds eliminate those concerns for investors who want to own gold bullion. These funds trade on the stock exchanges and can be bought and sold during the trading day. The unit of purchase is one-tenth of an ounce of gold, and the price of a share in the fund is about one tenth of the spot price of an ounce of gold. The names of two of the exchange-traded funds are StreetTRACKS Gold Shares and iShares Comex Gold. StreetTRACKS Gold Shares trade on the New York Stock Exchange under the symbol GLD. iShares Comex Gold trades on the American Stock Exchange under the symbol IAU.

Each of these two funds is managed by a trust that buys gold bullion and stores it in a bank vault. The managers of the trusts make book entries of each transaction, but there is no actual delivery of gold to the purchaser. This is similar to the book entry system for stock purchases where there is no delivery of stock certificates. When an investor wants to sell his or her gold, he or she initiates a sell order to the New York or American stock exchanges and a credit in the appropriate amount is entered to the seller's account with the brokerage. If you decide to buy an exchange-traded gold fund, note that it will not pay dividends.

MINING GOLD

The three phases of gold mining are exploration to discover deposits, development of the infrastructure to extract ore from the deposits, and processing the ore to produce bullion gold. Exploration requires trial drilling to discover potential deposits and confirmation drilling to determine the amount, location, and depth of the ore. The extraction of the ore is done from the surface or from underground mines. Producing the gold can be done by mechanical methods or by the less costly process of heap leaching with a weak cyanide solution to separate the gold from the crushed ore.

By means of extensive drilling, the engineers and managers of each mining operation estimate how much gold is in the deposits. The result is a statement of proven reserves and probable reserves. The larger these reserves are, the more valuable the properties. From the point of view of an investor looking for a long-term investment, the amount of gold that can be extracted at a low cost should be enough to keep a mine operating at a profit for at least seven years.

HEDGED GOLD SALES

Some mining companies negotiate contracts with banks to sell some of their projected gold production at prices available on the futures market. The point of this hedging forward is to obtain a contract with a price higher than is currently available on the spot market. If the price of gold falls after the contract is in force, the mining company gets the contracted price when the gold is sold and avoids losing the difference. But if the price rises during the time period of the contract, the amount of money the mining company receives when the hedged gold is delivered may be less than it could have received from the sale of that gold at the spot price.

POTENTIAL RISKS

Some mining companies have to deal with events and conditions that raise costs, including strikes by miners, floods and gas explosions in the underground mines, landslides in the surface mining operations, claims to property rights by local residents, opposition from environmentalists, and bureaucratic delays in issuing permits. The challenge for mining companies is to deal with these conditions and troublesome events in an effective manner while producing gold at a low cost per ounce.

ABOUT MINING COMPANIES

A mining company that has only one mining operation in an unfriendly country is in jeopardy if the local government decides to demand larger royalty payments or nationalize the mine. A mining company with mines located in several different countries is better able to continue operations if a local government decides to assert ownership over a mining operation.

Open pit mining allows for quicker production than constructing underground mines. Cyanide heap leaching is the most efficient method of extracting the gold from the ore. A company that can produce gold at a cost per ounce that is much lower than the current price of gold on the market is an attractive investment. A company that hedges the sale of more than 10 percent of its annual production is taking an unnecessarily large risk of losing income if the price of gold rises significantly.

A SELECTION OF COMPANIES

Tables 7-1, 7-2, and 7-3 show three lists of mining companies that can be bought on stock market exhanges. You may want to research these companies and decide if any are suitable for your portfolio.

The first group (Table 7-1) consists of high-tier producers having more than 50 million ounces of gold in proven and probable reserves.

TABLE 7-1

High-Tier Producers

Name of Company	Symbol	Approximate Reserves
Barrick Resources	ABX	100,000,000 oz.
Newmont Mining Company	NEM	92,000,000 oz.
Goldfields, Ltd.	GFI	70,000,000 oz.
Anglo Gold Ashanti	AU	52,000,000 oz.
Freeport McMoran	FCX	51,000,000 oz.

TABLE 7-2

Mid-Tier Producers

Name of Company	Symbol	Approximate Reserves
Harmony Gold	HMY	40,000,000 oz.
Royal Gold	RGLD	15,000,000 oz.
Yamana Gold	AUY	12,000,000 oz.
Centerra Gold	CG-T*	11,000,000 oz.
Agnico Eagle	AEM	11,000,000 oz.
Randgold Resources	GOLD	11,000,000 oz.

*Traded only on the Toronto Stock Exchange

TABLE 7-3

Low-Tier Producers

Name of Company	Symbol	Approximate Reserves
Iam Gold	IAG	9,000,000 oz.
Kinross Gold	KGC	8,000,000 oz.
Meridian Gold	MDG	7,000,000 oz.
Eldorado Gold	EGO	5,000,000 oz.

The mid-tier companies in Table 7-2 have between 10 and 50 million ounces of gold in proven and probable reserves.

The companies in the low-tier group (Table 7-3) have between 5 and 10 million ounces of proven and probable reserves.

Note: All reserves are subject to change. Many of these companies also have other mineral deposits such as silver, copper, zinc, lead, etc.

DECISION CONSIDERATIONS

Investors considering the purchase of gold should compare the advantages and disadvantages of owning an exchange-traded fund versus holding stock in a company that mines gold. Buying shares in an exchange-traded fund is a bet that the price of gold will rise in the future based on the relationship between supply and demand. The amount of profit from this ownership will be directly proportional to the increase in the price of gold. The political, environmental, and social problems that might affect a particular mining company would not be a matter of concern. If mining companies run into operational problems and produce less refined gold, this deficit would reduce the supply, to the benefit of investors in the exchange-traded funds.

But if the price of gold rises, the prices of stocks in the companies free of problems and operating efficiently will rise at a faster rate because the prices of gold mining companies' stocks are leveraged to the price of gold. Any rise in the price of gold increases the value of every unhedged ounce of reserves each company has. Similarly, every drop in the price of gold decreases the value of each company's unhedged reserves because the leverage works in both directions.

When faced with these considerations, some investors take a balanced point of view. They buy stock in a mining company they believe is well managed and whose mines are located in places relatively free of interruptions to production. They also buy some shares of an exchange-traded fund to have a balance between owning gold bullion and owning shares in a gold mining company.

The final decision should be based on your convictions and concerns. If you are confident there is negligible danger from terrorists, governmental mismanagement, inflation, or disease pandemics, there is no need for you to buy gold. But if you are worried about these potential disasters, you will probably feel more comfortable with some shares of an exchange-traded gold fund and/or a gold mining company.

If you do decide to invest in gold, the amount should be between 5 percent and 10 percent of your portfolio. If you feel strongly that the dangers are real and imminent, you might want to have an even higher percentage. If you believe the dangers are exaggerated, you should stay near the 5 percent level. In either case, you will have some insurance to protect yourself against geopolitical and financial problems.

TRACKING A GOLD FUND

If you decide to invest in gold, it is prudent to monitor the status of your investment by means of the charts available on finance.yahoo .com. Enter the symbol of the stock or the exchange-traded gold fund in the search slot and click "GO." Then select "Technical Analysis" from the menu at the left and click on "200" in the row of moving averages. Scroll down to the chart you have made. Check to see if the price (in blue) is trading persistently above the moving average (in red). See Chart 6-1 for an example of the desired relationship. If you see a favorable relationship, an investment in the stock or fund is potentially profitable. This chart should be checked at least once a week. If the price should drop through the moving average and you have more than 10 percent of your assets invested in gold, it would be appropriate to sell a portion of your holdings. When deciding how much to sell, retain the amount that will make you feel protected against the uncertainties of the times we live in.

8

DIVERSIFYING TO LIMIT RISK

INTRODUCTION

The purpose of investing is to improve your financial condition. But if you make no effort to protect yourself by controlling the level of risk, you may lose money. By diversifying over a variety of investments, you can lower your level of risk and obtain some protection against negative trends and events.

The last section of this chapter presents a sample portfolio diversified across five asset classes: stocks, bonds, real estate, gold, and international investments. After reading this chapter and reviewing the sample portfolio, you will have a basis for deciding how to diversify your own investments. You should then chose the method that is suitable for you.

DIVERSIFYING AMONG STOCKS

One of the simplest forms of diversification is to buy the stocks of companies in different industries (for example, organic foods, assisted-living facilities, electric utilities, homeland security, Internet search, natural gas producers, household items, storage facilities, pizza chains, and drug retailers). Since each of these businesses is different from all the others, by buying one stock from each type of business, you would have a diversified group of 10 stocks.

INDEX FUNDS

Another method of diversifying is to purchase an index fund that includes a wide variety of stocks. For example, the S&P 500 Index contains 500 stocks of the most widely held and actively traded stocks. The S&P Midcap 400 Index contains 400 stocks of medium-sized companies. The S&P Smallcap 600 Index represents 600 stocks of small companies. One of the easiest ways to diversify your stock holdings is to buy shares of an index fund that tracks one of these indexes. Or to get a broader range of representation, you could buy shares in each of three funds that track these three indexes.

MUTUAL FUNDS

There are thousands of mutual funds. Some of them specialize in one type of stock, such as utilities, oil producers, technology, blue chips, real estate, financial services, health care, emerging markets. Others hold companies grouped by size: large, medium, small, and very small. Some have companies selected for potential growth or for being undervalued. Others call themselves "balanced" because they hold several asset classes. You could choose to buy shares in the type of mutual fund that diversifies among the part of investments that have most appeal to you. The prospectus of each fund lists the types of investments the fund intends to hold, and quarterly reports show the specific holdings. Because of the wide variety of mutual funds, many investors choose one or more to help them achieve the goal of risk control through diversification.

CLOSED-END FUNDS

Some closed-end funds are diversified among stocks from many different countries. Others invest in bonds issued by foreign governments. Some hold real estate investment trusts or other specialized investments. One way to diversify with closed-end funds is to buy more than one type. Another way is to buy a fund that invests in companies from a variety of industries or in a variety of bonds. The closed-end fund section of *Barron's* magazine lists 14 different types of these funds.

Closed-end funds can be traded like stocks. Many of them offer high yields and some can be bought at a discount to their net asset value. Before buying any closed-end fund you should learn which specific types of investments the fund holds and determine if it is diversified in a manner that is suitable for you. An indication that a fund is well diversified is that it has no more than 2 percent in any one investment. Owning a selection of diversified closed-end funds is an approach used by some investors to control risk.

NOTES AND BONDS

The U.S. government issues notes and bonds in a wide range of durations from a few days to 30 years. All are backed by the full faith and credit of the government and are exempt from state taxes. States and jurisdictions within the states issue municipal bonds that are backed by the state, a county, a municipality, or revenue from an entity such as a toll road or bridge. The interest from municipal bonds is not taxed by the federal government. Corporations issue their own bonds and pay a wide range of interest rates based on their credit status. Those with the highest credit ratings pay the lowest rates of interest, and those with the lowest credit ratings pay the highest rates of interest. Portfolios that are diversified from a conservative perspective are likely to have some government or corporate notes or bonds.

REAL ESTATE

A home is a place to live and it is also the most costly investment most people make. Purchasing stock in a real estate investment trust is another way to invest in real estate. The value of these trusts fluctuates with the market prices of the properties they own and the amount of rents they collect. Over the long term, prices in the real estate market have risen, and real estate has been one of the most rewarding investments. The real properties contained in real estate investment trusts can add the potential for high income and capital gains to a diversified portfolio.

PRECIOUS METALS

Gold and silver are candidates for inclusion in a diversified portfolio because they provide some degree of protection against physical and financial disasters, inflation, terrorist attacks, and disease pandemics. Investing in precious metals can help control the level of risk from these types of problems. Holding an exchange-traded precious metals fund also eliminates the risks associated with owning individual mining companies. (See Chapter 7, "Potential Risks" section.)

CASH EQUIVALENTS

Money market funds are a convenient way to have cash available when it is needed. They pay a low rate of interest so they are not an appropriate place to hold a large percentage of your assets for a lengthy period. However, during a bear market money market funds can preserve your capital by providing a safe haven from the severe declines many stocks will have. When the market bottoms out, having cash available provides the opportunity to buy as a bull market begins.

DIVERSIFICATION CONSIDERATIONS

The major factors to consider in deciding how to diversify are your current stage in life, your earning power, your investment objective, and your tolerance for risk. Here are some suggestions based on these factors.

For the young businessperson with an investment objective of large capital gains and a high tolerance for risk, the following mix of investments can be adjusted to meet his or her particular objective and needs:

> A diversified group of growth stocks: 50 percent
>
> A diversified growth-oriented mutual fund: 30 percent
>
> A diversified real estate investment trust fund: 20 percent

For the middle-aged person with a medium tolerance for risk seeking capital gains and reliable income flow, the following types of holdings should be considered:

> A diversified growth-oriented mutual fund: 30 percent
>
> A real estate investment trust fund paying a high dividend: 30 percent
>
> A diversified closed-end fund paying a high dividend: 20 percent
>
> A national municipal bond fund paying a high dividend: 20 percent

For a risk-averse retired person with the objectives of preserving capital and receiving a reliable income flow, the following conservative investments should be considered:

> U.S. bonds with maturity dates spread from one year to 30 years: 50 percent
>
> A national closed-end municipal bond fund purchased when long-term interest rates are high: 30 percent
>
> A closed-end fund managed actively for high income: 20 percent

A SAMPLE DIVERSIFIED PORTFOLIO

This section shows how an investor might create a diversified portfolio of different types of investments. A diversified portfolio is composed of individual stocks, funds, and trusts. Each of these investments can be traded on the stock exchanges whenever they are open. Note that this type of portfolio can produce very positive returns during a bull market, but would likely decline during a bear market. Therefore, the best time to create this type of portfolio is at the end of a bear market. Also note that the listing of these investments does not constitute a blanket recommendation. Each investment should be evaluated for suitability to your individual financial situation and in relation to your level of risk tolerance.

Company/Fund Name	Symbol	Investment Category
Aqua America	WTR	Water Utility

Comment: This is the largest water utility in the United States. It has shown persistent growth in earnings. It provides fresh water and waste water services in several states and plans to expand by buying local municipal water utilities in additional states.

Sunrise Senior Living	SRZ	Assisted-Living Facilities

Comment: This corporation owns 40-plus facilities providing independent, assisted living, skilled nursing and rehabilitation services in the United States, Great Britain, and Germany. Approximately 90 percent of the residents are paying from private funds or with the aid of long-term care insurance policies. As the average age of retirees increases, the demand for the services provided by residential communities will grow.

Toyota Motors	TM	Automobiles

Comment: This is a fast-growing, very profitable automobile manufacturing company. It has a reputation for high quality and produces a wide variety of motor vehicles. It sells them in Japan, North America, and Europe.

PepsiCo	PEP	Soft Drinks

Comment: PepsiCo is best known for its many popular brands of soft drinks, but it also sells a variety of snack foods, cereals, pasta and rice meals, and bottled spring water. The demand for these products continues to increase.

eBay	EBAY	Internet Auctions

Comment: This the most popular worldwide online auction company. It has millions of users and devoted customers, some of whom operate home businesses through their postings on eBay. This service provides sellers the opportunity to make profits by selling items they no longer want, and gives buyers the ability to buy a huge variety of items that may not be available in their local stores.

Colgate-Palmolive	CL	Personal Products

Comment: This company is best known for its personal care products such as soaps, shampoos, and toothpaste. But it also sells fabric conditioners, cleaners, bleaches, and pet foods. It has operations in North America, Latin America, Europe, Asia, and Africa.

streetTRACKS Gold	GLD	Precious Metals

Comment: This is an exchange-traded fund. Each share in the fund represents one-tenth of an ounce of gold. The gold is stored in a bank vault and is registered in the name of the investor. This is a convenient way to own bullion gold. The fund does not pay a dividend.

Equity Residential Properties	EQR	Real Estate

Comment: This is a real estate investment trust. It owns and collects rents from more than 198,000 multifamily property units geographically dispersed over 32 states. This trust trades as a closed-end fund and pays a dividend of about 5 percent.

ACM Income Fund	ACG	Federal Government Bonds

Comment: This fund invests principally in U.S. government bonds and government sponsored agency obligations. It trades as a closed-end fund and pays a dividend of approximately 8 percent.

Eaton Vance Income Trust	EVN	Municipal Bonds

Comment: This trust invests in investment-grade municipal bonds issued by more than 30 states and local governments. The bonds are issued to raise funds to build toll roads, hospitals, housing, and water and sewer facilities. This trust trades as a closed-end fund and pays a dividend of approximately 7 percent.

BlackRock Global Opportunities Equity Trust	BOE	World Equity Funds

Comment: This trust invests primarily in securities issued by corporations around the world. The fund holds investments in more than 20 countries. The trust trades as a closed-end fund and pays a dividend of approximately 10 percent.

This collection of assets from five different investment categories provides reliable income flow, risk control through broad diversification, and the potential for capital gains. Now that you have reviewed the various ways diversification can be achieved, you are in a position to select a group of investments that will keep you in your comfort zone.

9

STOCKS TO BUY AND HOLD

INTRODUCTION

You may have concluded from the preceding chapters that it takes some time and effort to manage a portfolio through bull, bear, and range-bound markets. You may not have the time or be willing to do the research required for investing in short- and intermediate-term investments. If this is your situation, you may prefer to select a group of diversified stocks to buy and hold for a long-term period of more than a year. This chapter provides guidelines for finding some companies in less cyclical businesses, whose stocks generally fluctuate less drastically than others that are more sensitive to changing economic conditions. The listing of stocks presented in this chapter does not constitute a recommendation because only you can decide which investments are suitable for you.

STOCK SELECTION GUIDELINES

Here are the guidelines to help you in the selection process. Refer to Chart 9-1. This chart shows a stock price that is trending upward at approximately 20 degrees, a rate that is sustainable over the long term. Its 200-day moving average is following the stock price up at a similar angle of ascent. The most important feature of this relationship is the space between the stock price and its moving

CHART 9-1

Ideal Stock Price and Moving Average Relationship for Buy and Hold Investor

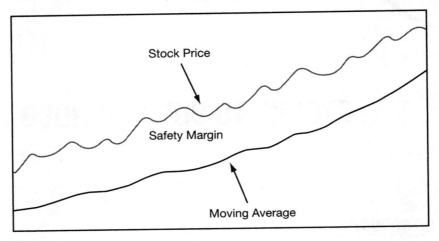

average. This type of gap, when maintained, shows what the stock price has done in the past and provides some indication that this rate of price appreciation can be carried forward. The space gap between the stock price and the moving average is a safety margin. So long as the gap persists, it is safe to hold the stock.

The stock price pattern shown in Chart 9-2 is not ideal, but it is positive because it is rising at a pace that can produce a significant capital gain over the long term. At times the price comes down toward the moving average and then rises some distance. The inability of the price to maintain a gap between it and the moving average indicates that demand for the stock is not steady. You should consider buying a stock with a pattern like this one only if you can't find any with the relationship shown in Chart 9-1.

Angles of ascent from 10 to 30 degrees are more sustainable and involve less risk than higher angles. This is because there is less participation by day traders and momentum players who are looking for a quick profit and have little interest in the company as a long-term investment. Angles of ascent of about 5 degrees or less are sustainable, but they do not provide a sufficient rate of return after inflation and other costs are subtracted from any gain.

CHART 9-2

Acceptable Stock Price and Moving Average Relationship for Buy and Hold Investor

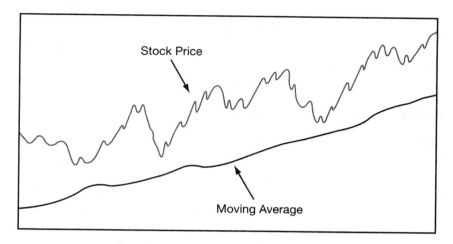

CHART 9-3

When to Sell a Long-Term Holding

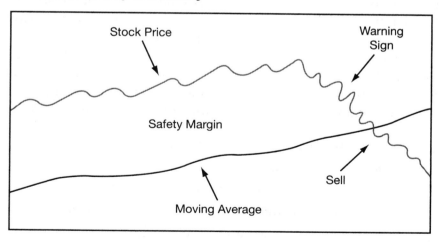

Refer to Chart 9-3. After you have bought a stock you hope will continue rising for the long term, it is necessary to monitor its performance. The ability of the price to remain above the 200-day

moving average is the critical factor. You should check the relationship at least once a week. If the price has been consistently above the moving average, a sudden decline toward the average is a warning sign the upward momentum is lessening. If the price declines through the moving average, the momentum has changed from up to down. Hopefully, this development will not materialize until you have a capital gain when you sell.

STOCK SELECTION PROCEDURE

Now that you know the significance of each pattern, you can get started in the search for 10 stocks that could be worth holding for the long term. In the following section you will see several types of businesses listed along with some companies in each business. These companies have extended growth records. They provide products and services needed by individuals and businesses, and they sell them at prices that produce good profits. Many of them have copyrights on brand names that have high recognition and are trusted by a loyal group of customers. These are some of the reasons for concluding they are good investments for the long term. To build a diversified portfolio, you should choose just one company from each of 10 of the 26 groups listed below.

Here is the method by which to select each of the 10 stocks. Review the description for each type of business. If you agree the long-term potential of that business is promising, select the company you believe is the best of the group and follow this procedure:

Note the symbol of the company's stock.

Go to finance.yahoo.com.

Enter the symbol into the search slot and click "GO."

From the menu on the left, select "Technical Analysis."

From the range of time periods, select "2y."

From the choice of moving averages, select "200."

Scroll down to review the stock chart you have selected. It shows the stock price in blue and the moving average in red.

Select it for your group of 10 stocks if the price and moving average relationship is similar to the one in Chart 9-1.

Note: If you can't decide which company to select, pick two whose chart patterns are positive. Note the symbols and go to finance.yahoo.com. Enter one of the symbols in the search slot. When the display comes up, select "Technical Analysis" from the menu on the left. From the time periods listed, select "2y." Then click on "200" to get the moving average. In the "Compare" slot, enter the symbol for the other company. Click on "Compare" and scroll down to see the relative peformance of the two stocks. Review this chart to decide which stock is the best performer in relation to the moving average and the other stock.

After you have made your decision, return to the listing of businesses and repeat the selection procedure until you have 10 diversified stocks.

Note: If you try this selection procedure during a quickly declining bear market, you will probably not be able to find stocks that qualify for long-term investing. In this situation, as funds become available, buy general obligation municipal bonds paying a high rate of interest and collect the income until the bear market in stocks is over. Since bear markets do not usually last more than 18 months, the maturity date of the bonds should be between 1 and 2 years in the future.

SELECTING COMPANIES

The list below shows the approximate dividend yield and price-to-earnings ratio for each stock as of the date of publication. The price-to-earnings ratio (P/E) is obtained by dividing the price of the stock by the earnings per share. Thus a stock with a price of $10 per share that earns $1 per share has a price-to-earnings ratio of 10, shown simply as 10. Price-to-earnings ratios are usually between 15 and 25 during a bull market. Price-to-earnings ratios should be compared within an industry or type of business. Companies with lower price-to-earnings ratios are generally thought to be more reasonably priced than companies with higher ratios. But if a company is increasing its earnings faster than its competitors, a higher ratio is justified.

1. *Nondurable household products.* These companies sell the household items purchased for every home. They have the well known brand names that make them more appealing than lesser known products. The demand for the items these companies sell is consistent and growing because they have many practical uses within our homes. The main competition to these brand-name products comes from less well known brands that are marketed at lower prices. As long as consumers prefer the better known brands and are willing to pay higher prices for them, these companies will maintain their dominance and profitability.

Company Name	Company Symbol	Dividend Yield (%)	P/E Ratio
Clorox Corporation	CLX	1.8	21
WD-40 Company	WDFC	2.6	17
Energizer Holdings	ENR	0.0	14
Colgate-Palmolive	CL	2.1	24

2. *Mining metals.* These companies provide the raw materials and commodities that industrial economies need to support manufacturing the products wanted by modern societies. They mine copper, aluminum, lead, zinc, nickel, titanium, etc. These materials are required to build cars, trucks, airplanes, ships, trains, highways, and bridges to meet our need for transportation and mobility. They are also used to construct homes and other structures that provide sites for living, working, entertainment, and all other aspects of modern existence.

Company Name	Company Symbol	Dividend Yield (%)	P/E Ratio
Rio Tinto, plc	RTP	1.5	14
BHP Billiton, Ltd	BHP	0.8	16
Freeport-McMoRan	FCX	2.2	12

3. *Water utilities.* These companies collect, filter, and deliver drinking water to consumers. Industries that require water in their

production processes are dependent on these services. These companies also collect and dispose of wastewater in a sanitary fashion. They perform these services on a contract basis for cities and suburban and rural communities. Their main competition comes from the bottled water producers over which they have a huge pricing advantage. Since water is basic to survival, and many people cannot affort the cost of bottled water, the community water utilities provide an essential service for the general population.

Company Name	Company Symbol	Dividend Yield (%)	P/E Ratio
Aqua America	WTR	1.8	40
York Water	YORW	2.5	33
American States Water	AWR	2.4	22

4. *Assisted living.* People are living longer, and as they lose their physical abilities, many of them prefer to have someone else maintain and clean their living quarters, prepare their meals, etc. These residential facilities also provide a social situation far superior to living alone in one's old age. The on-site staff is available to provide assistance when needed, which provides a feeling of security. The large baby boomer generation is reaching retirement age so the demand for these services is likely to increase. A major cost of running these facilities is maintaining the proper staff. So long as the pool of available workers is large enough to keep staffing costs under control, these facilities will be profitable.

Company Name	Company Symbol	Dividend Yield (%)	P/E Ratio
Sunrise Senior Living	SRZ	0.0	25
Manor Care	HCR	1.5	27
Brookdale Senior Living	BKD	2.8	N/A

5. *Book publishers.* Hundreds of millions of children around the world have read the Harry Potter series of books, which was published in many languages. This unprecedented phenomenon has created a huge surge of interest in reading. As these children age, they will be reading for enjoyment and information. Publishers are also making electronic versions of books available on the Internet to

a worldwide audience of readers. As the literate population of the world grows, the demand for the services provided by these publishers will increase. Recognizing and cultivating this global market available through the Internet will be important to the success of these companies.

Company Name	Company Symbol	Dividend Yield (%)	P/E Ratio
McGraw-Hill Companies	MHP	1.4	25
Pearson plc	PSO	3.4	14
Courier Corp.	CRRC	1.3	21

6. *Homeland security.*   The informal and nontransparent nature of some international financial transactions make it extremely difficult for the authorities to track and stop the flow of money to the terrorists. As they become better financed and more sophisticated in their methods, it will be critical to our security to use improved technology to defend against them. These companies produce equipment to detect biological, radiological, chemical, and nuclear contamination. They also develop systems to identify individuals by digital, facial, and ocular features and store this information in a data base for reference. These types of personal data storage and retrieval systems can detect a terrorist who has assumed a false identity. The demand for the products and services being developed by these companies will increase if the terrorists continue in their intentions to damage our country.

Company Name	Company Symbol	Dividend Yield (%)	P/E Ratio
L-3 Communication	LLL	0.9	20
American Science	ASEI	0.0	20
SRA International	SRX	0.0	33

7. *Weight control.*   Our population is gaining in average weight, and the incidence of obesity is increasing every year. Obesity often results in diabetes, and over 18 million Americans have this disease. This illness has many consequences such as eye problems and malfunction of the kidneys, nerves, and heart. Poor circulation can lead to amputation of feet and other physical problems. People

with diabetes must have their blood tested daily to determine levels of sugar in the blood. In view of all the ailments associated with obesity, the demand for the services of weight control companies is projected to grow in the years ahead.

Company Name	Company Symbol	Dividend Yield (%)	P/E Ratio
Reliv International	RELV	0.9	30
Ediets.com	DIET	0.0	50

8. *Casual footwear.*   Casual footwear manufacturers produce a wide variety of comfortable and stylish shoes, boots, sandals, and sneakers. The popularity of these alternatives to formal shoes has grown steadily in recent decades. They are a part of the life style of young folks, but are worn by all age groups. Expensive sneakers have become a status symbol for teenagers, and many youths own several pairs. These manufacturers and merchandisers provide a wide variety of footwear for special purposes like hiking, basketball, running, walking, tennis, soccer, etc. Many people who work at jobs requiring them to stand all day wear casual footwear instead of dress shoes.

Company Name	Company Symbol	Dividend Yield (%)	P/E Ratio
Nike	NKE	1.4	15
Skechers	SKX	0.0	23
Payless ShoeSource	PSS	0.0	30

9. *Tobacco products.*   Despite the negative publicity for smoking cigarettes, many young people still take up the habit. Once the addiction has taken hold, it is extremely difficult to escape. Very few smokers can give up their craving for the satisfaction they receive. Smoking is a global pastime and is becoming more popular in undeveloped countries. Many men find relaxation in smoking cigars and pipes, and some believe it is less unhealthful than smoking cigarettes. Because of the strength of the smoking habit, manufacturers have been able to raise the prices without losing customers. Class action suits against the cigarette makers have created some financial problems, but these companies manage to maintain a high level of profitability.

Company Name	Company Symbol	Dividend Yield (%)	P/E Ratio
Altria	MO	4.5	14
Reynolds American	RAI	4.7	15
Carolina Group	CG	3.8	13

10. *Public storage facilities.* These companies benefit from a low cost of maintenance since once built and rented to the public, there are only occasional visits by the renters to deposit or retrieve items. As retired couples sell their large homes and move into apartments, they need a place to store their excess possessions so the demand for storage space will continue to grow. So long as company officials only authorize new construction when more capacity is needed, the demand and supply relationship between rental space available and demand for that space will remain favorable. Profit margins are high, and since they operate as real estate investment trusts, the dividends to the investor are 90 percent of profits or higher.

Company Name	Company Symbol	Dividend Yield (%)	P/E Ratio
Public Storage, Inc.	PSA	2.6	40
Shurgard Storage	SHU	3.5	N/A
Sovran Storage	SSS	5.1	28

11. *Bookstores.* The Harry Potter book series has introduced the young generation to the pleasures of reading. As this group matures, their reading interests are likely to spread to nonfiction because of the requirement to be knowledgeable in this information-based society. These bookstore chains have become much more customer friendly by adding services such as beverages and snacks. They have also provided tables and chairs to give customers a place to sit, read, and relax.

Company Name	Company Symbol	Dividend Yield (%)	P/E Ratio
Barnes & Noble	BKS	1.4	20
Books-A-Million	BAMM	2.7	21
Borders	BGP	1.7	17

12. *Electric utilities.* These companies are dominant in their geographic areas and supply the electricity that every home and business needs. The competition from alternate sources is on a minor scale. The number of customers paying bills directly from their bank accounts is growing. This method of payment is convenient for the buyer and reduces the cost of collection for the utilities. As demand for electric power grows, these companies can look forward to higher profits for the foreseeable future.

Company Name	Company Symbol	Dividend Yield (%)	P/E Ratio
Exelon	EXC	2.8	49
TXU Corporation	TXU	2.8	20
Hawaiian Electric	HE	4.6	17

13. *Transportation services.* These companies provide truck or rail transportation for apparel, appliances, auto parts, chemicals, food stuffs, furniture, metal products, refined petroleum products, rubber, textiles, lumber, and miscellaneous items. Deliveries are made locally, regionally, and countrywide.

Company Name	Company Symbol	Dividend Yield (%)	P/E Ratio
C.H. Robinson	CHRW	0.9	39
Swift Transportation	SWFT	0.0	18
J.B. Hunt Transport Services	JBHT	1.4	19

14. *Food and drink.* These companies produce and sell the foods and drinks people need to have every day. This steady consumption provides a reliable flow of revenue. Since these are the necessities of life, the companies that produce them can maintain high profit margins.

Company Name	Company Symbol	Dividend Yield (%)	P/E Ratio
Panera Bread	PNRA	0.0	43
Flowers Foods	FLO	1.4	32
Corn Products	CPO	1.2	23
Hain Celestial	HAIN	0.0	37
H.J. Heinz	HNZ	2.8	21
PepsiCo	PEP	2.0	25

15. *Casual dining.* These restaurants provide a family friendly atmosphere where the parents and children can enjoy the type of meals they like. In many families, both parents work and don't have the time or inclination to prepare meals and clean up afterward. Eating out in low-cost restaurants is convenient. The waiters and waitresses make most of their compensation from tips so the salaries for the staff are minimal. Each restaurant has its own specialty of tasty meals and desserts, which ensures a steady stream of revenue from loyal customers. These restaurant chains have stores located in areas where the diners live.

Company Name	Company Symbol	Dividend Yield (%)	P/E Ratio
CKE Restaurants	CKR	0.9	10
Domino's Pizza	DPZ	2.0	20
Darden Restaurants	DRI	1.0	21

16. *Natural gas producers.* These companies are domestic explorers, producers, and distributors of natural gas to fuel the production of electricity and heat homes and businesses. As one of the cleanest, most environmentally friendly forms of energy production, natural gas usage is growing steadily in the United States. When oil is more expensive, some commercial energy users have the option of switching to natural gas. Until more nuclear plants are built, natural gas will be a cleaner source of energy. The demand for natural gas is expected to exceed supply for the foreseeable future.

Company Name	Company Symbol	Dividend Yield (%)	P/E Ratio
ONEOK	OKE	3.5	7
OGE Energy	OGE	4.2	15
El Paso	EP	1.2	N/A

17. *Household essentials.* These are the practical items found in every home. They have high recognition brand names familiar to millions of consumers. They are relatively inexpensive and durable and it would be difficult to get along without them. Among the many items available from these companies are products for infant

care; feminine hygiene; grooming; protection from the sun; cosmetics; kitchen gadgets; childrens' educational toys; preparing, cooking, and storing food; house cleaning; tools; permanent markers; pens; draperies; blinds; and high chairs and strollers. In short, everything needed to deal with the daily requirements of our modern lifestyle.

Company Name	Company Symbol	Dividend Yield (%)	P/E Ratio
Newell Rubbermaid	NWL	3.2	27
Whirlpool	WHR	1.8	15
Black & Decker	BDK	1.8	13

18. *Biotechnology companies.* These are leading companies in the biotechnology business. They conduct extensive research in cellular and molecular biology to discover new ways of treating and preventing diseases. They make and market multiple products for a variety of medical problems. They have effective business models and have increased their revenue and earnings steadily in recent years. The broad spectrum of medical treatments they provide should keep them profitable in the years to come.

Company Name	Company Symbol	Dividend Yield (%)	P/E Ratio
Genetech	DNA	0.0	70
Novartis AG	NVS	1.5	25
Gilead Sciences	GILD	0.0	35

19. *A/C, Heating, and refrigeration.* These companies provide indoor temperature control for our homes and businesses. They allow us to be warm in winter and cool in the summer, and they make the equipment to refrigerate stored foods so they remain fresh. These companies do business internationally and help the citizens of developing countries enjoy the comfortable lifestyle. The need for the systems and equipment they produce is worldwide and growing. As the demand for indoor climate control and refrigeration increases, these companies should remain profitable for the foreseeable future.

Company Name	Company Symbol	Dividend Yield (%)	P/E Ratio
Lennox International	LII	1.4	15
United Technologies	UTX	1.5	20
American Standard	ASD	1.7	18

20. *Pizza companies.* Pizza pies are one of the most popular foods among all age groups. These companies produce many varieties to please everybody's taste including vegetarians. By choosing the right size and thickness, one pizza can feed a small family. The convenience of having it delivered is another feature that makes pizza so popular. Overseas sales are the fastest growing part of the business and the size of the potential market in China is much larger than the domestic market. It appears there is much growth ahead both domestic and international, before supply can catch up with the universal appeal of, and demand for, the pizza pie.

Company Name	Company Symbol	Dividend Yield (%)	P/E Ratio
Papa John's	PZZA	0.0	25
Domino's	DPZ	2.0	16
California Pizza	CPKI	0.0	28

21. *Coal producers.* These companies mine and sell coal to industry for the production of energy in the form of electricity. The supply of coal in the United States is predicted to last at least 200 years at the current rate of consumption. Selling coal is a profitable business because of the problems with other methods of power generation. Some examples: dwindling available resources of natural gas that result in high prices, opposition to constructing nuclear plants because of safety concerns, lack of refinery capacity that makes oil for power generation expensive. This cost advantage for coal in comparision to the other major methods of generating power gives the producers a competitive edge and contributes to their continuing profitablility. As the current efforts to make burning coal less detrimental to the quality of air succeed, this will add to the attractivenes of coal as a means of producing energy.

Company Name	Company Symbol	Dividend Yield (%)	P/E Ratio
Peabody	BTU	0.4	34
Consolidated Energy	CNX	0.6	14
Arch Coal	ACI	0.5	70

22. *Railroad shippers.* Railroads are the only practical way to ship many heavy or bulk items. The amount of coal being transported to locations where it is burned is increasing because of price advantage over other forms of fuel. The railroads are also getting more business as the process of globalization continues. Shipments arriving at our ports must be transported to all sections of the country, and most of this is done by rail.

Railroad companies are using technology to move their cargoes more efficiently by requiring fewer car changes from train to train, better routing, and eliminating much of the delay time during the trips. Consequently, profit margins have been increasing and the railroads are becoming high-quality investments.

Company Name	Company Symbol	Dividend Yield (%)	P/E Ratio
Norfolk Southern	NSC	1.2	17
Union Pacific	UNP	1.3	23
Burlington Northern	BNI	1.0	20
CSX	CSX	0.8	19

23. *Canadian companies.* The supply of crude oil in the ground is declining steadily as industrial nations increasingly use more each year. There are huge deposits of tar and oil sands in Canada. Technological developments are making the extraction of oil from these sands practical, and Canadian energy companies are extracting and marketing this oil. The earnings of these companies should increase as the market for this oil expands.

Company Name	Company Symbol	Dividend Yield (%)	P/E Ratio
Canadian Natural Resources	CNQ	0.5	25
Petro-Canada	PCZ	0.7	16
Suncor Energy	SU	0.4	25

24. *Waste management.*   We produce mountains of waste every day and these companies collect, process, and dispose of it. Fortunately, some of it is recyclable so that it can be converted into usable products. The services these companies perform are essential to maintaining our communities in sanitary condition. The demand for these services is consistent throughout all seasons, which allows these companies to develop profitable business models.

Company Name	Company Symbol	Dividend Yield (%)	P/E Ratio
Waste Management	WMI	2.4	18
Allied Waste	AW	0.0	25
Republic Services	RSG	1.4	25
Waste Connections	WCN	N/A	22
Covanta Holdings	CVA	0.0	40

25. *Aerospace/defense.*   These companies are developing and operating the aerospace systems so essential to the defense of our country. The government places a very high priority on providing them with the financing they need to produce weapons and intelligence-gathering systems that allow our armed forces to have a strategic advantage over enemies. The requirement for these systems is expected to grow for the foreseeable future.

Company Name	Company Symbol	Dividend Yield (%)	P/E Ratio
Boeing	BA	1.4	25
Lockheed Martin	LMT	1.6	18
Northrop Grumman	NOC	1.9	17
Raytheon	RTN	2.0	23

26. *Food products.*   These companies run agricultural businesses that produce the crops from which our food products are made. These are essential items for our meals such as wheat, corn, soy, rice, oats, barley, peanuts, oil, seeds, etc. These food stuffs also comprise much of the feed for the livestock from which we get our beef, ham, pork, lamb, poultry meats, and eggs.

Company Name	Company Symbol	Dividend Yield (%)	P/E Ratio
Archer-Daniels-Midland	ADM	0.9	25
Bunge Ltd	BG	1.1	15
Conagra	CAG	3.2	21

Cautionary Note

Dividend yields and price-to-earnings ratios are as of the date of publication. To get current yields and price-to-earnings ratios go to finance.yahoo.com, enter the stock symbol in the search slot, and click "GO." The summary chart that appears contains these data items.

HOW TO FOLLOW UP

It will be necessary to do some follow up on the group of 10 stocks after they have been purchased. You should check each stock price weekly to see if any of them decline through the moving average. If this type of negative change in momentum occurs, the right course of action would be to sell the stock. The issue of what to do with the proceeds presents you with some questions to resolve and decisions to make.

Did the stock you sold lose its upward momentum because of an event or condition that affected the prospects of that particular company? Or can the cause of the decline be ascribed to the beginning of a bear market? If it appears the momentum loss is specific to that company, you can return to the list above and select another company to replace it.

On the other hand, if you decide the cause of the stock's decline is that a bear market is starting, the next question is, Will it be short and shallow or long and deep? If you believe the market decline will be short lived, you can continue your buy and hold strategy if your financial condition outside of the market is strong. But if you feel insecure financially or are worried about the scope of the bear market, it is appropriate to adopt a more conservative posture. You could switch to a defensive portfolio by following the guidelines presented in Chapter 5, "Suggested Portfolio Content" section.

To implement the change in strategy, you would use the proceeds from each sale of stock to acquire the elements of the conservative portfolio. You would then stay invested in the bonds, preferred stocks, and cash until it is evident the bear market has ended.

Note: Reading all of Chapter 5 will help you to decide if a bear market is starting and will provide information on how to select appropriate bonds and preferred stocks.

CHAPTER

10

PITFALLS TO AVOID

INTRODUCTION

Investors in the market are subject to a wide variety of influences that can produce emotional reactions of various intensities. A strong bull market can make investors feel hope, pride, or greed. The fast decline caused by a bear market can produce anxiety, fear, and panic. When these emotions take over, some investors make counterproductive decisions and suffer large losses.

In addition to the emotional impact of the dramatic price swings of bull and bear markets, other factors play a role in producing emotional reactions. Failing to assess the risk in each investment in a conscientious manner can produce negative feelings and stress. For example, investors should consider how the risk factor changes from one type of investment to another as indicated below.

Individual common stocks: highest risk

Mutual stock funds: less risk than individual stocks

Preferred stocks: less risk than mutual funds

General obligation municipal bonds: less risk than preferred stocks

U.S. government bonds: least risk

Another factor that can raise the negative emotional component of investing is overcommitting. Each investor must be careful to limit the money invested in equities such as stocks and stock funds to an an amount within his or her comfort zone. Emotional reactions elicited by going outside that zone can be very strong and lead to errors in judgment and tactics. Descriptions of several of these pitfalls are presented below.

TACTICAL PITFALLS

One of the most common tactical errors of investors is hoping to catch the bottom in a long decline of a stock price. When a stock is in a downtrend, there is no way to predict where it will end. If the price topped out at 90, it looks cheap at 50, and maybe that will be the bottom. It looks even cheaper at 40 and 30 and 20, etc. Rather than try to guess where the bottom is, the better tactic is to be patient and wait until you see completion of a bottoming pattern such as a rounding bottom, a double bottom, or inverted head and shoulders.

BUYING NEAR THE TOP

As a stock price rises steadily, it becomes more and more attractive. The momentum players keep pushing the price upward, and many investors have huge paper profits. For some investors, the lure of a popular stock is difficult to resist. But because of its popularity, a stock may become greatly overpriced. At some point, there are very few buyers willing to pay the high price while there are many stockholders happy to sell. When this condition develops, the path of least resistance is downward, and investors who buy near the top are in a precarious position. Be wary of a stock that has had a steep rise and the consensus opinion is that it will keep rising.

BUYING A FLAT LINER

Stocks that have been much higher sometimes drop to a very low price and stay there, give or take a small amount. The price pattern is basically flat and it appears to be making a floor. A flat price pattern means that investors have lost interest in the company, and the company management doesn't know how to correct the problems. When, if ever, they will figure out how to revive the company is unknown. Investors who buy this type of stock are likely to waste a lot of time waiting for something good to happen. In some cases, the situation deteriorates into bankruptcy and the owners of the stock may be holding a worthless asset. Buying a stock that has been flat lining at a low level for a long time is indulging in unjustifiable hopefulness.

TRADING THE TAPE

Some investors watch a financial program and notice frequently traded stock symbols on the live ticker tape at the bottom of the screen. If they see a price rising rapidly, they may decide to enter a buy order in order to get the stock while it is going up. Buying a stock on the basis of seeing its symbol rising in price on active trading, but without any knowledge of the company represented by the symbol, is a tactical error. In the absence of research, there's no way of knowing whether the rising price is justified or whether day traders and momentum players are the main buyers of the stock. When the stock loses its upward momentum, the active traders will abandon it quickly and the investor who bought impulsively is left with a stock that will likely drift lower over time.

TRADING FREQUENTLY

The convenience and low cost of each transaction on the Internet induce some investors to trade too often and not take the time to do informative research. The primary beneficiaries of active trading are the brokerage companies because of the large amount of commissions that are generated. Buying and selling frequently without the benefit of research raises the cost of investing and does not allow a reasonable chance of making successful investments.

BUYING PENNY STOCKS

Some low-priced stocks that do not qualify for listing on a major market exchange can bought for less than a dollar. Some speculators commit the error of believing they can't go any lower. Unfortunately, they can not only go lower, but some of the companies they represent go bankrupt. Stocks that trade for pennies are usually priced so low because the companies they represent have very little value.

BORROWING MONEY

Some banks and most brokerages will lend you money to buy stocks, and some brokerages will let you pay for purchases with a credit card. This is an expensive way to play the market. From the beginning, you will be paying interest on the loan so that reduces any profits you might make. If you are in a margin account and the stock price goes below the limit set by the brokerage, you will get a margin call and if you can't come up with the additional cash, they can sell your stock and you will have to suffer the loss.

SELLING SHORT

If you watch the market for a while you may see a stock going up a lot and conclude it is drastically overpriced. You may then decide to sell it short in the hope of making a large profit. But if the momentum players keep pushing the price above the point where you went short, you may have to cover your short sale at a large loss. In theory, there is no limit on the amount you could lose. This is one of the riskiest tactics, and an investor who wants to keep losses within manageable limits should avoid using it.

TRADING "AT THE MARKET"

One of the most common errors investors make is buying or selling "at the market." While this order ensures that the transaction occurs, it often results in an unfavorable price. When purchasing a stock at the market price, you give away your right to negotiate the best deal for yourself. Instead you agree to accept the price the seller wants. When selling at the market price you agree to accept the price the buyer wants. No matter how eager you are to buy or sell a stock, the best way to do this and get a favorable price is to enter a limit order. That way you enter the negotiation on an equal footing with the seller or buyer. To put these situations in perspective, remember that the seller is probably as eager to sell as you are to buy, and the buyer is probably as anxious to buy as you are to sell. Usually you can get your limit orders filled at prices you have determined rather than letting the other party to the transaction get the price he or she wants.

BUYING ON TIPS

When investors gather and socialize, tips are often passed along. Unfortunately, there is usually no way to check on the validity of the information since it has not been published. If you are closer to the end of the tip line than to the beginning, you could be paying too high a price. If you are impressed by the story told by the tipster, check it out. If there's no way to check, keep your money in your wallet.

BUYING ON MEDIA HYPE

Stocks that have been making large gains attract attention. Commentators in the media play a role in pushing these stock prices higher by giving them favorable publicity. It's very tempting to jump on the bandwagon and go along for the ride. But when today's darling of the investment community falls out of favor, demand dries up and the price may decline rapidly. Popularity can fade at the slightest hint of bad news because expectations are so high. Ironically, buying a very popular stock too frequently results in a loss.

BUYING ON THE PHONE

Many investors are solicited on the phone by their brokers. Sometimes the broker calls because he or she has a quota of a brokerage inventory to sell. If this is the case, the broker's desire to sell the assigned shares is not necessarily in your best interest. If you feel you are being pressured to make a purchase, one way to deal with the situation is to tell the broker to send some literature on the investment. This gives you time to do your own research, review the information you receive from the broker, and decide whether the purchase would be an appropriate addition to your portfolio.

Solicitation phone calls may also come from brokers employed by other brokerages. These brokers are making cold calls to acquire new clients. You can also deal with these brokers by asking them to send some literature on the investment. In either of these situations, you should not submit to pressure to make an investment on the basis of a phone call.

BUYING ON RUMORS

"Buy on the rumor, sell on the news." This is one of the favorite statements of professionals in the stock market. If the professionals in the business are doing this, it would be futile for most investors to follow this advice because the pros are likely to hear the rumor and get the news first and sell quickly. Then the nonprofessionals working at their day jobs only see the decline in price at the end of the day when the prices are lower.

Aside from the above problem, there are other reasons not to buy on a rumor. Many rumors of positive developments are inaccurate, exaggerated, or completely untrue. Buying on the basis of rumors is making a bet on the reliability of something that is inherently unreliable. Some rumors are simply speculation that has been passed along and changed in the process. Perhaps you remember the party game where people stand in a line and the first person whispers something to the second person and the message is passed along. The reason this game is fun to observe is because the message as stated by the last person has little resemblance, if any, to the original statement, and everyone has a good laugh. But betting money on rumors is no laughing matter because losing money is no fun at all.

BUYING ON CONSENSUS OPINION

When everybody agrees on the prospects for an investment, it's time to be skeptical. When the media, the professionals, and the general population of investors all recognize the merits of a company or the bright future of an industry, why should anyone doubt the majority opinion? The reason for questioning the conventional wisdom is that demand for an investment tops out when everybody loves it. This means that tops are created by overwhelming positive attitudes and it's time to be taking profits rather than be a Johnny-come-lately. In general, the majority opinion may be right for the immediate future, but beyond that it is likely to be wrong. The best way to evaluate the correctness of a consensus opinion is to conduct your own research and come to a conclusion based on independent reasoning.

BUYING ON MESSAGE BOARD COMMENTS

Commenting about stocks on their message boards is a popular activity. Some of the participants own the stock and some have sold it short. Their comments are in line with their positions and cannot be taken as objective commentary. Comments like "Strong buy" and "Strong sell" are indicative of passionate opinions and feelings, and are not thoughtful recommendations. Do not buy or sell on the basis of suggestions or comments on the message boards.

BUYING WHAT YOU DON'T UNDERSTAND

It's a poor tactic to buy stock in a company whose business you don't understand. If you don't know how a company produces earnings, you won't know how various factors such as interest rates, the economic cycle, and competition might affect the prospects for the business. This lack of knowledge will leave you in the dark as to whether the company will prosper, stagnate, or fail as time passes. It is better to buy stock in companies that have simple, easy-to-understand business models that produce reliable earnings.

TRADING EMOTIONALLY

Hope is the driving force behind much investment activity. Investors risk their money hoping to be rewarded by an increase in their net worth. Without the potential of being rewarded for risks taken, there would be few investments made. Hopefulness is a positive influence as long as expectations are reasonable.

A low level of greed is motivational and can serve to keep investors participating actively and with enjoyment. But when greed gets out of control, it can be hazardous to an investor's financial condition. The investor who rides a stock up for a major capital gain and wants to sell at the highest point is letting greed take over. This type of investor holds on stubbornly in frustration when the stock drifts lower and wipes out much of the gain.

Another sign of uncontrolled greed is investing a large portion of a portfolio in one speculative stock with the desire to make a huge profit. The chances of this fantasy coming true are very small and the usual result is a loss of time and money.

Too much greed is also a factor when an investor always prefers risky trading tactics such as using the maximum amount of margin or selling a volatile stock short. Margin calls and short squeezes bring the overextended investor back to the reality that high-risk tactics can have dire consequences.

The emotion of fear can become the dominant feeling for some investors. Fearfulness becomes a factor when too much of an investor's assets are risked in speculative investments that decline unexpectedly. Speculating with more money than the investor can afford to lose may result in overwhelming fear. In the worst case, fear turns into panic when a stock price goes into a prolonged decline, and the investor sells out near the bottom.

ASSESSING RISK TOLERANCE

Learning how much risk you can tolerate well is not subject to a mathematical calculation. That knowledge only comes from the school of experience. To understand the basic concept of risk tolerance, use the following guideline. If your primary goal is to preserve the assets you have, you are risk averse. Your main challenge is to be able to take advantage of the capital gain opportunities available in a bull market. On the other hand, if you are mainly focused on finding opportunities to increase your wealth, you are risk tolerant. Your main challenge is to avoid high-risk stocks during a bear market. But whether risk tolerant or risk averse, you should stay within your comfort zone to avoid the financial losses that often go along with strong emotions.

11

BECOMING A SELF-DIRECTED INVESTOR

INTRODUCTION

This book has presented the foundation of information necessary for you to become a self-directed investor. This is important because you are the only one who has your financial interests as top priority. The professionals in the business often have other objectives, such as earning more commissions or fees, trying to sell an inventory of sponsored securities, implementing the instructions of management, or working toward a promotion. Using technical analysis gives you the capability of making your own decisions rather than depending on someone whose interests are not the same as yours. Independent, self-directed investing is the key to avoiding the problems that can arise from these potential conflict-of-interest situations.

Now that you know how to do your own research before making an investment, the next step is to find a broker who will act as your agent to facilitate your transactions in the market. The following sections describe some of the actions you can take to find a broker who will respect your independence and provide assistance to help you discover profitable investments.

FINDING A FULL-SERVICE BROKER

One way to find a broker is through the suggestion of a friend or business associate. If recommendations are not available, check your local telephone directory under the heading of "Stock and Bond Brokers." Look for one that is within a reasonable driving distance. It is important to meet face-to-face to determine if you can develop a satisfactory business relationship. During your telephone call make an appointment to visit the office. Your objective is to make sure you will be dealing with a reputable business and an experienced broker. Plan on having an extended conversation.

The first issue to explore during the interview is whether you can develop a sound business relationship with this person. This will be someone whom you want to represent you in making investments. After stating your financial objective, the size of your account, and your level of tolerance for risk, the broker should give a response showing an understanding of your situation and a willingness to help you achieve your goal.

Next you should explore the broker's approach to investing. How does the broker evaluate an investment? Does he or she use a technical or fundamental evaluation procedure, or a combination of the two? The answer should be one of those alternatives or some other information-based approach. If instead he or she just follows the brokerage's directions, that could result in a conflict of interest where the needs of the company are given higher priority than your requirements.

During the interview, state that you intend to develop your own ideas on investments, but will appreciate any help that is offered. The broker should react to this statement by indicating his or her availability to provide assistance. With this kind of responsive broker attitude, a mutually beneficial long-term relationship can be developed.

If you are satisfied with the meeting, ask for a copy of their cash account agreement and read it carefully. You should also ask for a copy of their commission schedule. If you feel the agreement and the commissions are reasonable, find out what is required to open an account and complete the paperwork.

If you have not been satisfied with the interview, leave without making any commitment. Later you can look for another brokerage in the telephone directory and repeat the interview process. With perseverance, you should be able to find another brokerage that meets your needs.

Before opening an account with any brokerage, you should call the National Association of Securities Dealers to make sure there are no transgressions in the broker's background. Their phone number is 1-800-289-9999. You can also go on line at www.NASD.com and get the same information.

MAKING THE TRANSITION

If your account is below $100,000, it is best to deal with a one-broker office. A broker who is in charge of an office is more likely to have sufficient experience to help you reach your financial goal. When you call an office, ask how many brokers work there. The more brokers there are, the more likely your account will be assigned to one who is less experienced. With an account above $100,000, you should make the point with the office manager that you want to have your account assigned to a more experienced broker.

In starting with any new broker, you should let him or her know you would appreciate information and suggestions about potential investments, but you will be the decision maker. The broker is your agent and you are justified in expecting efficient execution of your orders and a quick report of the details of the transaction.

INTERNET BROKERAGES

You may also want to open an account with an Internet brokerage if you don't already have one. The reason to have both types of brokerages is the flexibility you gain. A full-service broker can help you increase your knowledge of the market and act as a sounding board in regard to the investment ideas you originate. But when you do your own research and get no help from a full-service brokerage, you would execute your purchase through a discount brokerage on the Internet.

In selecting an Internet brokerage, there are factors to consider in addition to cost. Does the Internet brokerage provide a market entry platform that allows you to place your orders efficiently? Is it easy to understand and use? Does it have aids such as stock price charts to allow you to do a technical analysis? If you want information or assistance, is it available conveniently by e-mail or phone? When you call for help, do you have to wait on hold a long time before you are connected to a person in Customer Service? Will you get a confirmation of each transaction on hard copy if you want one? Do you get a competitive return on your cash balance? When you need to deposit or withdraw money, can it be done conveniently and safely?

STAYING WITH YOUR CURRENT BROKER

Perhaps you are content with your full-service broker if you have one. If so, you could expand your relationship with him or her by asking if technical analysis is a factor in his or her decision making. This could lead to a productive exchange of information if he or she is familiar with this approach. You could also discuss which phase the market is in and consider the best strategy for that phase. And when you both have time for an extended discussion, you could jointly review how well diversified your portfolio is and what could be done to improve it. By means of exploratory conversations like these you can make progress toward becoming a self-directed investor.

A sound long-term relationship with any broker is based on mutual respect and trust. Hopefully, your broker respects you and is trustworthy. However, you also have some obligations in the relationship. First, if your broker recommends an investment and, after doing your own investigation, you decide to buy it, it is proper to let him or her enter that order rather than do it yourself on the Internet. Second, make payments on time so your broker doesn't have to be a bill collector. Third, examine your monthly statements and clear up any questions you have. Fourth, get price quotes through the Internet unless you are preparing to make a transaction through the full-service brokerage. Fifth, make an appointment to meet with your broker a couple of times a year to maintain a good personal relationship. Sixth, continue toward the goal of becoming a self-directed investor so you can eliminate any conflict of interest from the relationship.

REWARDS OF SELF-DIRECTION

Becoming self-directed requires motivation, dedication, and self-confidence. These attributes will enable you to find your own investments and enjoy the pleasure of discovery. After you have become a self-directed investor, you will experience satisfaction and pride in your achievement and you will be in command of your financial future.

12

REVIEW EXERCISE

INTRODUCTION

This chapter provides an opportunity for you to determine how well you have learned to interpret the relationships between stock prices and their moving averages. Careful attention to these relationships provides information that will help you make profits in the stock market.

MAKING CAPITAL GAINS

In this section, there are seven pairs of charts. The question to be answered for each pair of charts is this: Which stock is more likely to make a large capital gain? The correct answer is on the page following each pair of charts, along with the reasoning for the choice.

REVIEW EXERCISE

Question 1

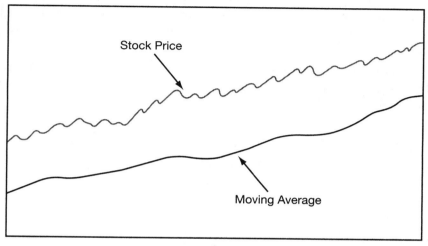

Stock Price

Moving Average

A

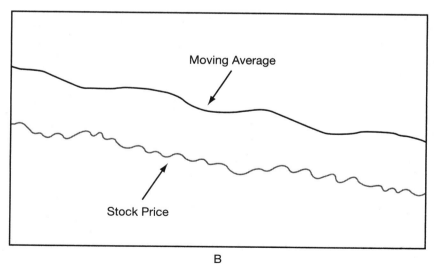

Moving Average

Stock Price

B

Answer to Question 1

Chart A shows the stock that is more likely to make a large capital gain. The price is moving upward and there is a wide gap between it and the moving average. The gap represents a safety margin and as long as this gap persists, the stock can be held for additional gains.

In Chart B the stock and its moving average are in downtrends. It is a self-defeating tactic to hold a stock in an established downtrend.

REVIEW EXERCISE

Question 2

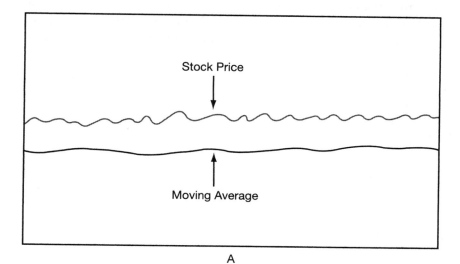

A

B

Answer to Question 2

The stock in Chart B is more likely to make a large capital gain for the same reason as stated in the answer to question 1. The stock price and moving average in Chart A are in a flat line formation which makes it unlikely a capital gain will be made by this stock.

REVIEW EXERCISE

Question 3

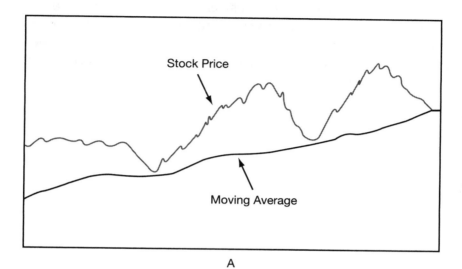

Answer to Question 3

The stock in Chart B is more likely to make a capital gain for the same reason as stated in the answer to question 1. The stock in Chart A is also trending upward, but its inability to maintain a space above the moving average is a warning sign that the momentum could change to the downside if the price goes down through the moving average.

REVIEW EXERCISE

Question 4

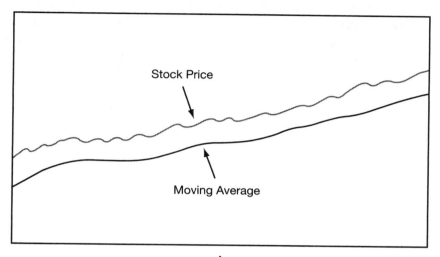

A

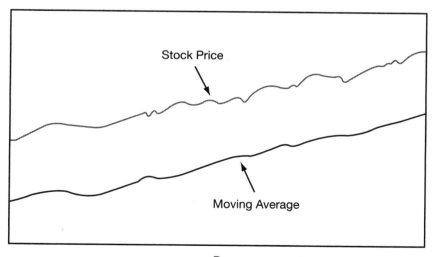

B

Answer to Question 4

The stock in Chart B is more likely to make a large capital gain because the gap between it and its moving average is wider than the one in Chart A. The larger gap is a more reliable indication the uptrend will persist. The narrower gap in Chart A provides a smaller safety margin which could vanish quickly.

REVIEW EXERCISE

Question 5

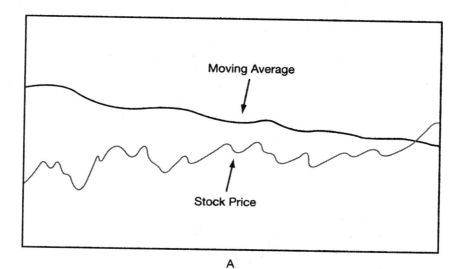

A

B

Answer to Question 5

The stock in Chart A is more likely to make a large gain. The price of the stock has just moved up through the moving average. This signals a change in momentum to the upside and provides a buy signal. The stock in Chart B is trending down and should be avoided.

REVIEW EXERCISE

Question 6

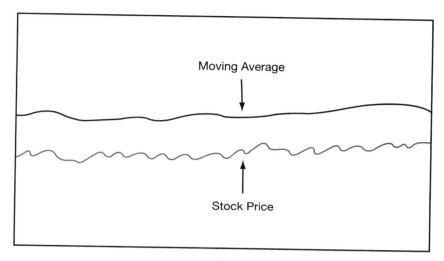

A

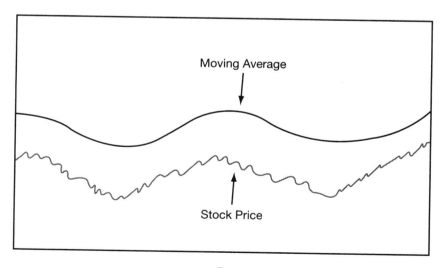

B

Answer to Question 6

The stock in Chart B is more likely to make a large capital gain. It has just completed a double bottom and could start a major uptrend from that pattern. The stock in Chart A is in a flat line formation. It would not be able to penetrate its moving average to the upside without some major good news.

REVIEW EXERCISE

Question 7

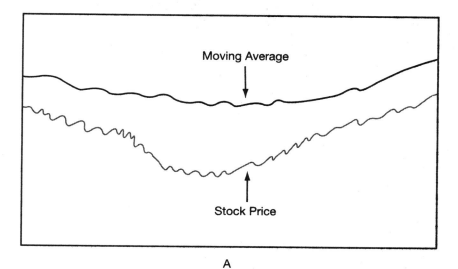

A

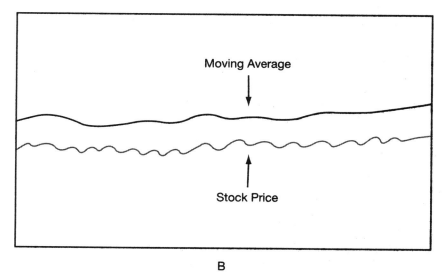

B

Answer to Question 7

The stock in Chart A is more likely to make a large gain. It has made a rounding bottom and has started an uptrend that could continue for the intermediate or long term. The stock in Chart B is flat, indicating investors don't see any prospect of better times ahead.

WHICH STOCKS TO AVOID?

In this section there are six pairs of charts. One chart in the pair shows a stock that is not likely to produce positive results. Knowing which investments to avoid is just as important as being able to identify winners, because buying the wrong stock can result in a loss of time and money. The question to be answered in regard to each pair is this: Which one should not be bought if your objective is to make a capital gain?

REVIEW EXERCISE

Question 8

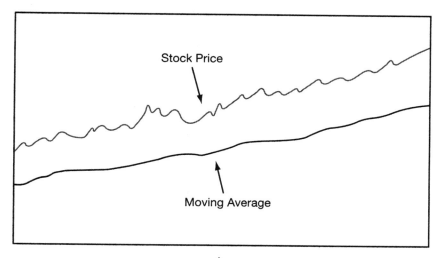

A

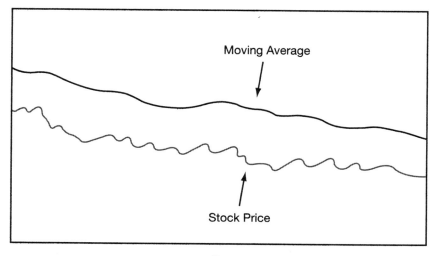

B

Answer to Question 8

The stock in Chart B should not be bought because it is in a down-trend. Since there is a large gap between the price and the moving average, there is little likelihood the trend will change in the foreseeable future.

REVIEW EXERCISE

Question 9

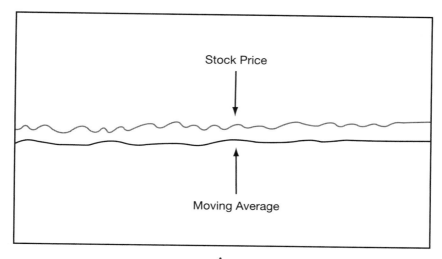

A

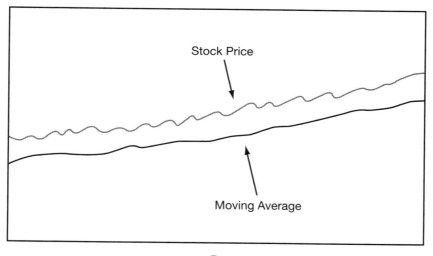

B

Answer to Question 9

The stock in Chart A should not be bought. It is in a flat line formation and the chance for a capital gain is nonexistent as long as this pattern persists. In addition, there is a chance the stock price will penetrate the moving average to the downside and start a downtrend.

REVIEW EXERCISE

Question 10

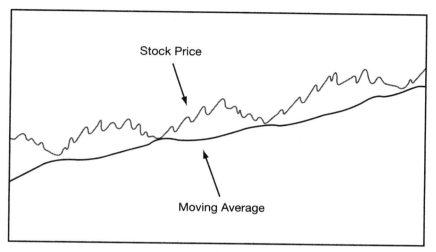

A

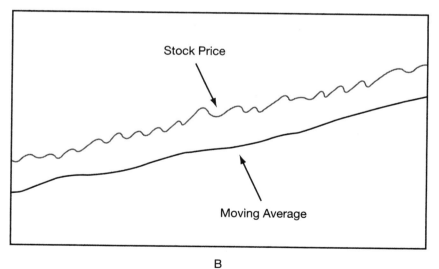

B

Answer to Question 10

The stock shown in Chart A should not be bought. The price is moving erratically and could penetrate the moving average to the downside on its next decline. A pattern like this indicates that mostly short-term traders are trading this stock and it does not appear to have the potential for large gains.

R E V I E W   E X E R C I S E

Question 11

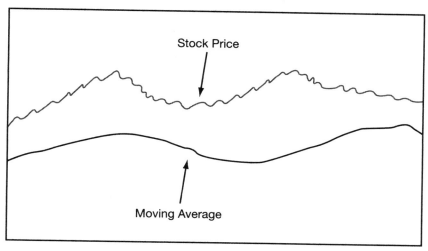

A

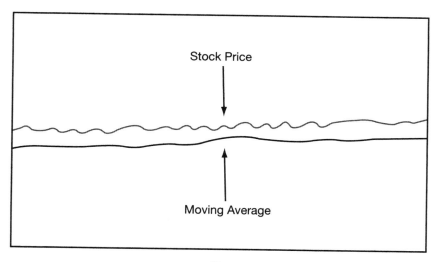

B

Answer to Question 11

The stock in Chart A should not be bought. The price has made a double top, which indicates a major move to the downside is very likely.

REVIEW EXERCISE

Question 12

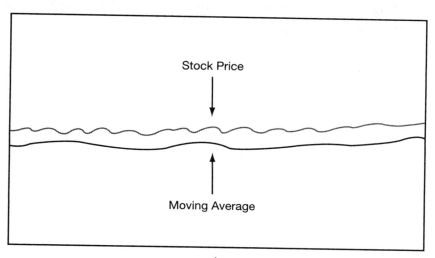

A

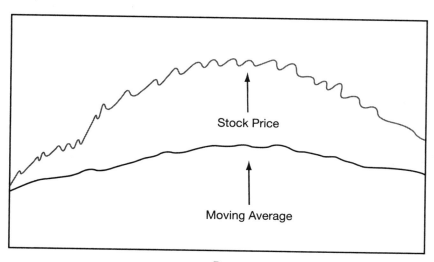

B

Answer to Question 12

The stock in Chart B should not be bought. The price has made a rounding top and, as in the preceding question, a major move to the downside is very likely.

REVIEW EXERCISE

Question 13

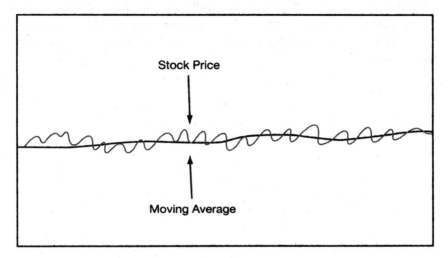

A

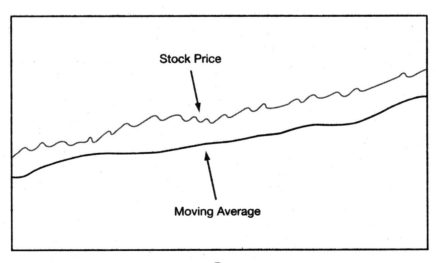

B

Answer to Question 13

The stock in Chart A should not be bought. This variation on a flat line formation is equally likely to resolve into either a downtrend or an uptrend. Before committing funds to an investment, you should look for a favorable pattern rather than one where the chance for a loss is 50 percent.

WHICH STOCK HAS MORE POTENTIAL?

In this section, there are three pairs of charts. Each chart shows a different relationship between the stock price and its moving average. With thousands of stocks to choose among, developing the ability to choose one that gives you the the higher return on your investment pays off greatly in the long run. The question to be answered in regard to each pair is this: Which stock shows the potential for a larger capital gain?

REVIEW EXERCISE

Question 14

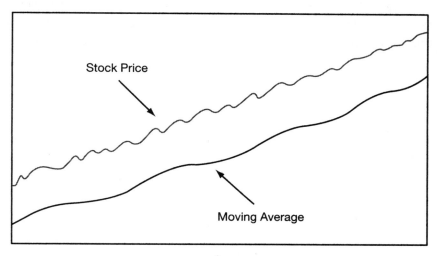

A

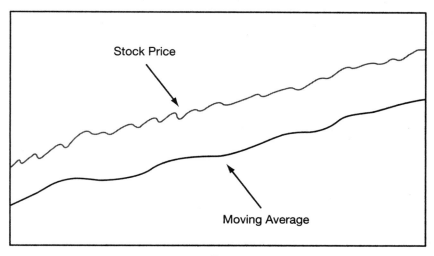

B

Answer to Question 14

The stock in Chart A has the potential for a larger gain. The stock price and its moving average are moving up at a higher angle of ascent than the one in Chart B. The longer these stocks are held, the greater the comparative gain for the stock in Chart A would be.

REVIEW EXERCISE

Question 15

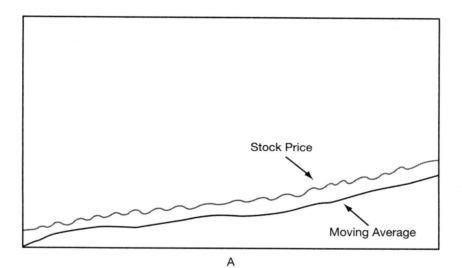

A

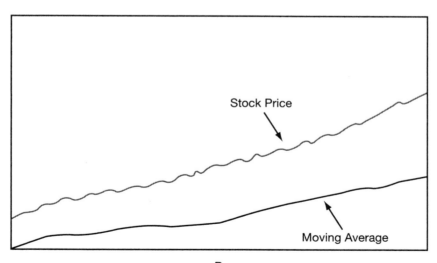

B

Answer to Question 15

The stock in Chart B has the potential for the larger gain. The angle of ascent is higher and the gap between the stock price and its moving average is wider. These features indicate the rise in price is likely to go further and faster than the price rise of the stock in Chart A.

REVIEW EXERCISE

Question 16

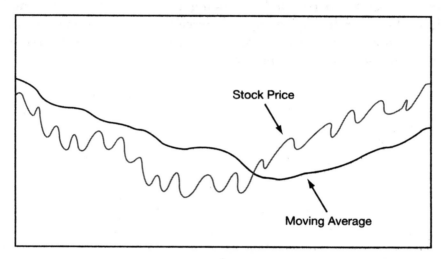

A

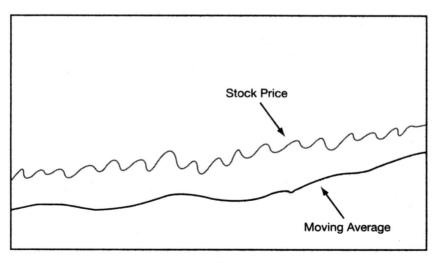

B

Answer to Question 16

The stock in Chart A is likely to produce the larger gain. The price of the stock has penetrated its moving average to the upside. This indicates a significant change in the price momentum from down to up. Although the price of the stock in Chart B is also trending upward, the angle of ascent is lower.

CHOOSING THE RIGHT TIME FRAME

In this section, there are three pairs of charts. Each chart shows a stock price and its moving average rising at an angle of ascent. The longevity of a rise in price is usually associated with the angle of the rise. Steep rises often have shorter life spans and the low-angle rises are generally more sustainable. You will improve your success ratio if you choose stocks that have characteristics in line with your temperament. If you want quick results, you will be more satisfied with stocks that have strong upward momentum and rise fast. If you are a patient person, you will more likely be content with a stock in a sustainable uptrend over the long term. If you are somewhere in between with respect to the time span of holding an investment, you should like those stocks that can make significant gains in an intermediate time frame.

REVIEW EXERCISE

Question 17

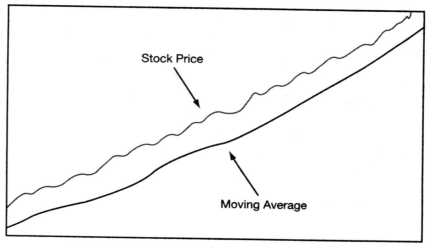

A

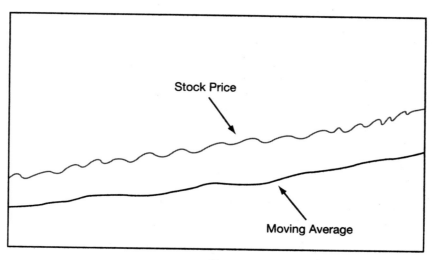

B

Answer to Question 17

The stock in Chart A should be purchased by investors looking for quick capital gains. The angle of ascent is approximately 35 degrees, which would produce a significant price rise in several months. The angle of ascent in Chart B is about 10 degrees, so the gain would occur at a much slower pace.

REVIEW EXERCISE

Question 18

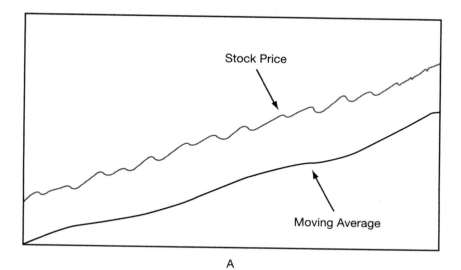

Stock Price

Moving Average

A

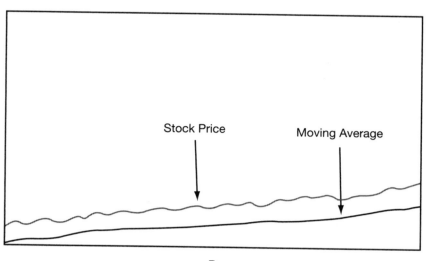

Stock Price

Moving Average

B

Answer to Question 18

The stock in Chart A should be purchased by investors seeking capital gains in the intermediate term. The angle of ascent is about 20 degrees, and this would provide an appreciable capital gain within a year. The angle of ascent of the stock price in Chart B is around 5 degrees and the return on investment would be minimal.

REVIEW EXERCISE

Question 19

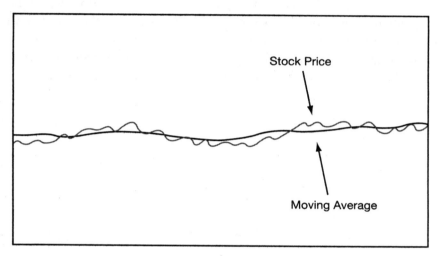

A

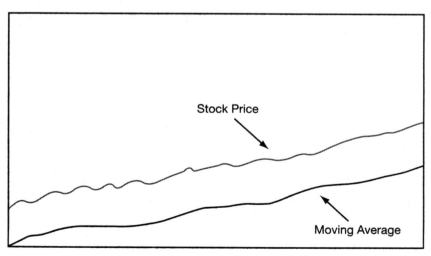

B

Answer to Question 19

The stock in Chart B is appropriate for the long-term investor. Angles of ascent between 10 and 15 degrees are sustainable for the long term. This type of stock performance is often associated with established companies that have shown their ability to make profits through all phases of the market and various economic conditions. Patient, long-term investors appreciate the steady progress of these stocks, which often pay good dividends.

ASSESSING RISK

Questions 20, 21, and 22 refer to the concept of risk tolerance. Each investment involves some degree of risk. Is your tolerance for risk high, medium, or low? It is important for you to be aware of your ability to tolerate risk and not exceed it in the purchases you make. By not surpassing your level of risk tolerance, you will be able to stay within your comfort zone where it is easier to handle the ups and downs that characterize stock prices.

Refer to the three pairs of charts that follow. Review each pair of charts and decide which shows the stock price and moving average relationship with the higher degree of risk.

REVIEW EXERCISE

Question 20

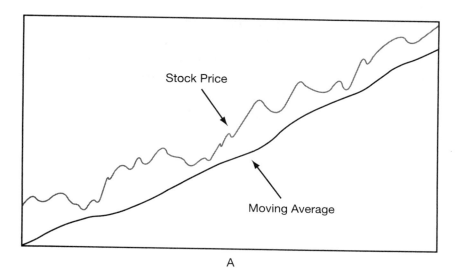

A

B

Answer to Question 20

The stock in Chart A has the higher level of risk. The price is show-ing more volatility and the angle of ascent is higher. High angles of ascent and excessive volatility indicate the participation of momen-tum players. These are nimble traders who usually have little or no interest in the nature or value of the company's business, and, in some cases, the only thing they know about the company is its stock symbol. These players buy a stock that is rising and sell it quickly when they are convinced the time has come for taking profits.

REVIEW EXERCISE

Question 21

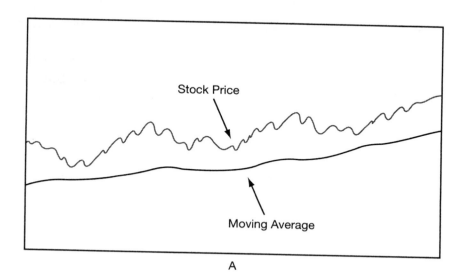

Stock Price

Moving Average

A

Stock Price

Moving Average

B

Answer to Question 21

The stock price in Chart B is making a head and shoulders formation and therefore has the higher level of risk. When this pattern is
completed, the stock price will probably descend to much lower
levels. Although the stock price in Chart A is volatile, the angle of
ascent is low and momentum players would not be attracted to this
situation. Both stocks have above-average levels of risk, but the
stock in Chart B is riskier.

REVIEW EXERCISE

Question 22

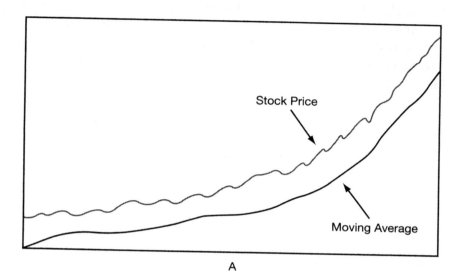

A

B

Answer to Question 22

The stock in Chart A is making a parabolic curve. The rise in price has accellerated and it is going almost straight up. Price rises of this extreme degree cannot be sustained and the subsequent fall is often as fast as the rise. The parabolic curve is the riskiest price pattern, and trailing stop loss orders are a way to salvage some profits. (See Chart 3-7.)

SAMPLE STOCK PORTFOLIO

Shown below is a sample portfolio of stocks. Each stock was selected on the basis of three criteria.

1. The stocks price was in an uptrend.
2. The price was above its moving average.
3. There was a gap between them that had lasted for at least four months.

For each stock, the company name, symbol, and price at the end of December 2005 are provided.

To determine how this portfolio has performed, enter current prices and calculate the percentage of gain or loss for each stock. If the shares of a stock have been split since the book was published, revise the initial price to reflect that split. Also, if the stock price has declined below its 200-day moving average, the stock should have been sold on the day that happened. The price on that date should be recorded instead of the current price. To find the price on the day the stock price fell through its moving average, first determine that date by creating a price chart with a 200-day moving average. After ascertaining that date, go to finance.yahoo.com and click on "Historical Prices." Enter that date in the search slot and use the closing price for that day.

SAMPLE PORTFOLIO GAINS OR LOSSES

Company Name	Company Symbol	Initial Price*	Revisions, If Any	Current Price†	Percent Gained (+) or Lost (−)
TETRA Technologies	TTI	15.26			
WD-40	WDFC	26.26			
Garmin Ltd.	GRMN	33.17			
Dril-Quip	DRQ	23.60			
West Pharmaceutical	WST	24.74			
Casual Male Retail	CMRG	6.13			
Allegheny Energy	AYE	31.65			
Archer-Dan.-Midland	ADM	24.66			
Carpenter Tech.	CRS	70.47			
Cameco	CCJ	31.66			

* Substitute split-adjusted price in the revision column if shares have been split.
† If stock price has declined below its 200-day moving average, substitute the price of the stock when that occurred.

158

B

GLOSSARY

Accumulation—Persistent purchases of a stock by knowledgeable investors who believe the shares are greatly underpriced. This activity takes place when a rounding bottom is being formed.

Annual Report—Each company listed on a stock exchange must publish an audited summary of its financial condition and operational results after the end of its fiscal year.

At the Market—One of the terms which can be used in entering a buy or sell order. It orders the broker to buy or sell immediately at the best available price.

Average Trading Volume—The average volume of trading over a period of time (usually three months). This figure is recalculated every business day to reflect the most recent time period.

Bear Market—A phrase used to describe a long-term downtrend in stock market averages as well as upward price movements that are short in duration.

Bottom Fishing—A phrase that describes a purchase during a long downtrend in which the buyer hopes to buy at the bottom price as it occurs. The chance of being right using this tactic is extremely low.

Bottoming Out—A process by which a major downtrend is converted into an uptrend. This change in direction can occur in one day by means of a breakout from a downtrend or in a key reversal day. Or it can develop over an extended time period in the form of a major bottoming pattern. See *Bottoming Pattern*.

Bottoming Pattern—There are three common patterns that occur at major bottoms: rounding bottom, double bottom, and inverted head and shoulders. However, there are also many ill-defined formations that can occur during a bottoming process.

Breakout—See *Downside Breakout* and *Upside Breakout*.

Brokerage—A company in the business of buying and selling stocks and bonds and other financial instruments. These companies act as agents for investors and traders.

Bull Market—A phrase used to describe an extended uptrend in the market averages as well as downward price movements that are relatively short in duration.

Business Model—The way the company conducts its business to produce earnings. From the investors' point of view, it should be clear how this is done. If the company has a reliable way of generating revenue, and the managers are able to keep costs under control, the business is being operated on a sound basis.

Buying on Margin—When you borrow money from your brokerage to buy stocks or to sell them short, you are trading on margin.

Call Date—The date on or after which a preferred stock or a bond may be called by the issuer.

Call Price—The monetary amount to be returned to the investor when a preferred stock or bond is called by the issuer.

Capital Gain—The amount of profit made on a completed transaction.

Capital Loss—The amount of loss incurred on a completed transaction.

Capitulation—A term used to describe mass selling of shares that occurs at the bottom of a bear market decline. The emotional component of this activity is one of despair or panic.

Cash Flow per Common Share—The dollar amount of revenue minus the dollar amount paid to holders of any preferred issues divided by the number of outstanding common shares.

Churn an Account—Excessive trading in an account that increases the broker's commission and disregards the customer's interests.

Closed-End Fund—A fund that issues a limited number of shares. These funds trade on the stock market and can be bought and sold the way individual stocks are traded.

Commission—This is a fee charged by brokerages to execute a financial transaction on behalf of a client.

Common Stock—The basic form of ownership in a public corporation that entitles the owner to voting rights and a proportionate share of common-stock dividends.

Consolidation—The price action of a stock that fluctuates in a random fashion for a period of several weeks or longer before beginning to move upward. This term is also used to describe a period when the market averages are stalled below a ceiling.

Continuation Formation—The pattern formed by the fluctuations of a stock price as it pauses during a bull market rise. The price enters the pattern from below and exits the pattern to the upside.

Cover a Short Sale—To sell a stock short, the shares are borrowed from another investor and sold with the promise to return them within a limited time period. Covering the short sale is the act of buying the shares back so they can be returned to the lender.

Cyclical Industry—An industry whose profits rise and fall in correlation with the rise and fall of the economy.

Day Trader—A person who watches the market on a computer and often makes one or more transactions within a business day.

Defensive Stocks—Stocks that resists the decline of a recession in the economy. These stocks have reliable earnings and usually pay dividends.

Demand—The total number of shares sought for purchase by all participating buyers. When this number is greater than the number of shares available from sellers, the price rises.

Discount—A security is bought or sold at a discount when the price is below its par or face value.

Discount Brokerage—A brokerage that provides trading services for lower commissions than those charged by full-service brokerages.

Discounted Purchase Price—The price paid by an investor who buys a preferred stock or a bond below its face value. This phrase also applies to a closed-end fund when it is purchased at a price below its net asset value per share.

Discretionary Account—A type of account where an investor gives control to the broker. The broker can then buy and sell without the prior approval of the customer.

Distribution—Persistent selling of shares by knowledgeable stock holders who are aware that prices are unjustifiably high. This activity occurs at the top of the bull phase in the market or in a stock.

Diversification—The spreading of investments among a variety of asset classes to reduce the overall risk level of the portfolio.

Dividend—The dollar amount paid to each common or preferred shareholder from the company's earnings.

Double Bottom—The price pattern formed when a stock price in a long-term downtrend reaches a bottom, rises from that level to a short-term top, goes back down to the previous bottom, and subsequently rises beyond the short-term top.

Double Top—The price pattern formed when a stock price in a long-term uptrend rises to a top, falls from that level to a short-term bottom, goes back up to the previous top, and subsequently falls beyond the previous short-term bottom.

Downside Breakout—A price drop below a support level or an uptrend line. The breakout is normally followed by a price move to lower levels.

Downtrend Line—A line drawn through two or more descending short-term tops.

Due Diligence—Conducting a serious examination of the value and timeliness of an investment.

Emerging Markets—This refers to countries that are evolving from an agrarian and/or resource based economy to one with developing industries and financial institutions.

Exchange-Traded Funds—These are funds that consist of shares in a popular market index such as the Standard & Poor's 500 or the NASDAQ 100. Other types of exchange-traded funds provide investors with the opportunity to own shares in a commodity or a basket of commodities.

Exponential Moving Average—An average calculated from a consecutive series of prices with extra weight given to the more recent prices. The line representing this average is shown in relationship to a history of the stock or fund prices it is derived from.

Full-Service Brokerage—A brokerage that provides advice, research information, and other services and charges relatively high commissions. Transactions are executed by the broker who is handling the client's account.

Fundamental Information—Details on company products, services, financial condition, competitors, and other factors affecting a company's prospects.

Futures Market—A market that allows participants to enter into contracts to buy and sell for specified future time periods.

General Obligation Bonds—Bonds that are backed by the financial resources of a state or municipality. They are the safest type of municipal bonds.

Globalization—The trend toward conducting business internationally.

Growth Company or Fund—A company or a fund that has above average prospects for increasing earnings over time.

Heap Leaching—The use of a weak solution of cyanide to extract gold from crushed gold ore. This is the most cost-effective method of extracting gold from the ore.

Hedging Forward—A contract to make a delivery of a commodity in a future time period. For example, a gold mining company signs a contract to deliver a certain amount of gold at a specified price in a future month in the current or future year.

Initial Public Offering—When a private company first gets listed on a stock exchange, it makes its initial offering of stock in the company through one or more of the commercial banks or brokerage houses that underwrite the distribution of the stock. The company is described in a prospectus for all interested parties to study. The shares are issued on an announced date and at a set price. As soon as the offering is completed, the shares can be traded by investors.

Intermediate Term—The time period from six months to one year.

Internet Brokerage—A brokerage company that does its business primarily through electronic means and facillitates transactions without the use of brokers.

Inverted Head and Shoulders—A major bottoming pattern composed of a bottom, another lower bottom, and a third bottom at a level approximate to the level of the first bottom.

Key Reversal Day—A day on which a stock price makes a new high, but closes with a loss on increased trading volume. The trend has now changed from up to down. Also, a day in which a stock price makes a new low, but closes with a gain on increased trading volume. The trend has now changed from down to up.

Limit Order—Placing an order to buy or sell at a specified price. If you are buying, a limit order puts a top on the price you are willing to pay, but also makes it possible for you to pay a lower price. If you are selling, a limit order puts a bottom on the price you are willing to take, but also makes it possible for you to receive a higher price.

Liquidation Value—The price at which a preferred stock is redeemed when it is called or matures.

Long Term—A period of time one year or longer.

Margin—This is the amount of money a brokerage is willing to lend to customers for the purpose of buying stocks or selling them short.

Margin Call—If an investor buys on margin and the stock price declines beyond a limit established by the brokerage, the broker calls the investor to request more money. If the investor does not wish to risk more money, the broker may sell the stock to prevent the loss from going too far. The investor must bear any losses involved in the transaction.

Market Index—A market index represents the composite price level of a group of stocks. For example, the Standard & Poor's 500 Index of stocks represents the price level of those 500 stocks as a group. This index is the most representative of the stock market because it contains the stocks that are most actively traded and widely held.

Message Boards—Locations on the Internet where e-mail messages are posted by the participants in the board. These boards are established and managed by Web sites. There is little or no supervision of the content of the messages. On the boards pertaining to stocks, many of the messages are either promotional or disparaging, depending on whether the person has a long or short position in the stock.

Microcapitalized—This phrase refers to the smallest publicly traded companies in terms of capitalization (the value of a company in terms of share price times the number of shares outstanding).

Momentum Player—An active trader who watches for a fast-moving stock. The player buys the stock with the intention of making a quick capital gain. This tactic is used by many market participants who watch the price action of stocks on their computers. Succeeding with this tactic requires access to a sophisticated trading platform connected to the Internet, a high level of experience, and excellent timing.

Moody's Corporation—A bond rating company that rates bonds from the highest (AAA) to the lowest (D).

Mortgage-Backed Securities—Some real estate investment trusts assemble mortgages into securitized packages. These packages are then sold to other investment companies which buy them for the income flow they deliver.

NASDAQ—This acronym stands for the National Association of Security Dealers Automated Quotation System. This market system is operated and regulated by the National Association of Security Dealers (NASD).

Net Asset Value per Share—The market value of a fund's portfolio of stock minus any liabilities, divided by the number of shares in the fund.

Objective—When used as an adjective, an objective decision is based on hard data and reliable information.

One Day Reversal—A change in the direction of a stock price trend. It is accomplished by a large movement in price accompanied by volume of trading that is many times more than the average volume.

Open Pit Mining—Mining a mineral from the layers of ore on, or just below, the surface.

Operating Profit Margin—This equals income from operations divided by total revenue. The higher this percentage is, the more efficiently the company is operating.

Overbought—This refers to a security that has become severely overpriced because of excessive demand from eager buyers.

Oversold—This refers to a security that has become severely underpriced because of excessive supply offered by anxious sellers.

Paper Loss—A loss that has not been taken, but remains as an item in an account.

Paper Profit—A profit that has not been taken, but remains as an item in an account.

Par Value—The stated value of a security.

Parabolic Curve—A charted price increase that accelerates until it is going almost straight up. This rate of increase cannot be sustained indefinitely. When the demand for the stock has been exhausted, the price usually falls sharply to much lower levels.

Portfolio—The collection of securities an investor accumulates to maximize return and keep risk to a comfortable level. The contents should be rebalanced as the market moves through the bull, range bound, and bear phases.

Preferred Stock—A class of stock that takes precedence over the common stock in regard to dividend payments. The issuer promises to redeem the stock at par value on the call date.

Premium Price—The price paid by a buyer who pays more than the par or face value of a security or the net asset value per share of a closed-end fund.

Price-to-Earnings Ratio—This ratio is the result of dividing the price of the stock by the earnings per share. For example, if the stock price is $10 and the company earns $1 per share, 10 divided by 1 equals 10. So the price earnings ratio is 10 to 1.

Probable Reserves—This phrase refers to underground resources that have been identified but have not yet been assessed acurately.

Profit Margin—A measure of company profitability calculated by dividing gross profits by sales. For example, gross profits of $1,000,000 divided by sales of $10,000,000 equals a profit margin of 10 percent (0.10).

Prospectus—An official document that gives a description of a company's business, objectives, risks, and other information of importance to an investor.

Proven Reserves—Underground resources that have been identified and quantified.

Pump and Dump—This is a tactic used by stock manipulators to get a quick profit. They use whatever method is available to praise a stock in the media and/or on the Internet to raise the price and then sell it to get the capital gain.

Range Bound—This term refers to a market that lacks the momentum to move up or down for an extended time period. In this condition the market index vacillates within a limited vertical distance.

Rebalance—To adjust the contents of a portfolio to meet the changing conditions of the stock market as it moves through bull, range-bound, and bear phases.

REIT—Acronym for real estate investment trust: a trust that owns real estate or mortgages on properties.

Relative Strength—This is a rating of a stock's price performance relative to the price movement of other stocks. A rating above 50 is a sign of relative strength. A rating below 50 is a sign of relative weakness.

Resistance Level—The price level from which a stock's price has declined in past attempts to penetrate it.

Risk Averse—This term applies to an investor who should only consider low-risk investments. A risk-averse investor who takes on too much risk and gets outside his or her comfort zone may experience extreme emotions that can result in unwise decisions.

Risk Tolerance—The level of risk an investor is willing and able to tolerate. To avoid stressful reactions, an investor should not exceed his or her level of risk tolerance.

Rorschach Test—A psychological test based on a variety of inkblot images. The inkblots are shown to a person and he or she is asked to describe what they see. Based on the responses, a psychologist makes an attempt to evaluate the subject's personality and temperament.

Rounding Bottom—The saucer shaped curve that develops when a downtrend in a stock price changes gradually to an uptrend.

Rounding Top—A curving top formation that develops as an uptrend is gradually converted into a downtrend.

Securities and Exchange Commission(SEC)—The federal agency that is responsible for regulating the actions of publicly listed companies.

Selling Short—This is the sale of borrowed shares with the hope the price will decline before the shares have to be purchased and returned to the lender. This is a very risky tactic since there's no limit on how high a stock price can go and the short seller may have to buy the stock back at a much higher price than when it was sold short.

Service Provider—A company that connects computers to the Internet and provides a variety of information services and access to thousands of Web sites for a monthly fee. This type of service is necessary for an investor who want to use an Internet brokerage.

Short Squeeze—This happens when a stock which is sold short by many speculators rises to price levels that make the speculators fearful and pressures them to buy back as the price rise continues.

Short Term—A time period from one to six months.

Simple Moving Average—An average calculated from a consecutive series of preceding daily closing prices.

Spot Price—The price to buy a commodity for immediate delivery.

Standard & Poor's Corporation—A company that maintains several market indexes and provides a variety of data services to the investment community. One of the important services it provides is the rating of bond issues from the highest (AAA) to the lowest (D).

Streaming Quotes—A live display on a portion of a computer screen that shows the changes in stock prices as they occur.

Supply—The total number of shares stockholders want to sell. When this number is larger than the amount investors want to buy, the price declines.

Support Level—The price level from which a stock has risen after declining to it one or more times.

Sustainable Angle of Ascent—Angles of ascent in the charted price of a stock of up to 30 degrees are sustainable over the long term.

Technical Analysis of Price Charts—A stock price chart provides a price record of all the trades in a stock. This record shows patterns that can be analyzed to arrive at implications as to future price direction.

Topping Out—A process by which a major uptrend is converted into a downtrend. This change in direction can occur in one day by means of a breakout from an uptrend or in a key reversal day. It can also develop over an extended time period in the form of a major topping pattern.

Trading Platform—This refers to the service provided by brokerages connected to the Internet. The platform presents information to assist the investor in making trading decisions.

Trailing Stop Loss Order—A sell order that follows the stock price up and is raised after each new high. When the stock price declines to the price specified in the stop loss order, it becomes an order to sell at the market price.

Underwrite—To have the authority and the responsibility to prepare for the issuance of a security and its sale to investors. The underwriting firm may assign portions of the security inventory to cooperating firms to help in the sale of the issue

Upside Breakout—A rise through a resistance level or a downtrend line. A breakout is normally followed by a price move to higher levels if the breakout is accompanied by a large increase in trading volume.

Uptrend Line—A line drawn through two or more ascending short-term bottoms.

Yield—The amount of return on a stock when dividends and capital gains or losses are added together. For bonds, it is the return on investment when interest and capital gains or losses are added together.

Zero Coupon Bond—A bond that has been stripped of its interest coupons and therefore pays no interest. This type of bond is bought at a discount, and the buyer receives the par value of the bond at maturity. The amount of return to the purchaser is dependent on the size of the discount when the bond is purchased. These bonds are a relatively safe investment because they are backed by the full faith and credit of the U.S. government.

C

HELPFUL WEB SITES

Descriptions of Internet Web sites are provided on the following pages. These sites were selected because they have a large amount of information in the form of charts, explanations, and definitions that can provide assistance in your self-education efforts. Much of the content of these sites is available without charge. Additional services are offered to those who register to become members and pay the fee charged by the site. You will find it worthwhile to review the sites to see how they can provide the objective information necessary for making sound investment decisions.

These Web sites present information that is kept current on a daily basis, and when the markets are open for business, price quotes are changed throughout the day. Millions of investors visit these sites daily through their personal computers, laptops, and wireless handheld devices. An investor who does not take advantage of the wealth of content available from the Internet is laboring under a competitive disadvantage. If you make the effort to learn what is available from these sites, you can become a self-directed investor who is able to find the important information required to invest successfully.

SUMMARY OF WEB SITE CONTENTS

The main helpful features of the Web sites listed in this appendix are provided below. Web site addresses are shown with the descriptions of the sites.

- For stock charts that can be customized to your needs, see Yahoo! Finance, ClearStation, Big Charts, or MarketWatch from Dow Jones. If one of these sites is down, the others can provide similar charts and information.
- For stock screeners that allow you to find stocks with the characteristics you want, see MSN Money, MarketWatch from Dow Jones, Yahoo! Finance, or Quantum Online.
- For the ability to store and retrieve your personalized stock charts, see Big Charts.
- For a comprehensive listing as well as descriptions of real estate investment trusts see the Web site of the National Association of REITs.
- For an objective, numerical rating of companies and a risk/reward evaluation of their stocks see MSN Money Web site.
- For an extensive lists of preferred and other stocks with specialized characteristics, see Quantum Online.

YAHOO! FINANCE WEB SITE

Web address: finance.yahoo.com

This home page gives a summary of the stock and bond market activities for the day, publishes several top news stories, and suggests several investment ideas. It also has a menu from which you may choose to see the most active stocks, the type of stocks of interest to you by means of a screener, and the news on various industries.

By entering a stock symbol in the search slot, you can access information on thousands of stocks and bond funds that can be customized to provide the technical information you want. The charts can be made to show different time periods (from one day to five years), simple and exponential moving averages (from 5 to 200 days), and comparisions of the charted price record of a subject stock to four other stocks and to three stock market indexes.

Fundamental information on companies is also available as follows.

A description of the company's business

The company's latest income statement

The balance sheet showing assets, liabilities, etc.

Current data on the company's cash flow

Information on size and profitability of competitors

Information on the company's major stockholders

Insider transactions in the company's stock

Record of dividends issued previously

Monetary compensation for managers

This site is well organized and provides comprehensive data and information on companies, stocks, and funds. It is an excellent starting point for researching any potential investment.

CLEARSTATION WEB SITE

Web address: www.clearstation.com

The home page of this site displays a variety of items. It names an outstanding stock as the "Clear Pick" of the day. It lists three "Hot Sectors" and five "Hot Industries," which are the outstanding performers for the week. Click on one of the "Hot Sectors," and the various industries within that sector are shown. Click on one of the industries, and the various companies in that industry are displayed by symbol. Click on a symbol, and a chart of the stock price is shown along with related technical and fundamental data.

Also shown on the home page is a list of 20 stocks presented under headings of "Record Price Break Outs," "Uptrends," "Over-Sold," "Analyst Upgrade," and "Community Favorites."

Enter a company's stock symbol in the search slot and the information available for selection includes "Profile and Fundamental Data," "Key Financial Ratios," "Reports by Analysts," "Earnings Estimates," "Record of Insider Trading," and "News Articles" on the company. In addition, there is a feature called

"Interactive Graph Tool." With this capability you can create a customized chart to show the frame of reference and information you
want, including the following items.

Length of time covered in the chart from 1 day to 10 years

Quarterly dividends paid and stock splits, if any

Quarterly earnings or losses

Three different lengths of moving averages

Direction of money flow in or out of the stock

Price momentum up or down

Relative strength compared to other stocks

Several other technical indicators

The customization features also allow comparisons of the stock
price performance to that of the Standard & Poor's Index and to
several other indexes. The multifaceted view presented by this Web
site is available for thousands of stocks and funds and makes
ClearStation a valuable information source for investors wanting to
do independent research.

STOCK CHARTS.COM WEB SITE

Web address: www.stockcharts.com

The home page of this site offers an option called "SharpChart."
After entering a stock symbol in the search slot, the price chart
shows the "Relative Strength Indicator," trading data for the day,
the stock price history for six months, a record of the trading volume, and the 50- and 200-day moving averages. During business
hours, the chart is updated continuously to show current trading
statistics.

Additional charts are shown under the heading of "Gallery
View." This display shows three charts. The first one is a six-month
chart with an indicator showing whether money is flowing in or

out of the stock during the period. The second one is a two-year chart with a 200-day moving average. This longer time frame gives you a larger perspective on the price trends and patterns. The third chart uses the point-and-figure charting style and gives an estimate of a price objective for the stock.

Another feature of this site, available at the home page, is their "Chart School" curriculum. The four subject matters presented are "Chart Analysis," "Indicator Analysis," "Market Analysis," and "Trading Strategies." When you have some time available, there is much to be learned from this comprehensive curriculum.

BIG CHARTS WEB SITE

Web address: www.bigcharts.com

The home page of this Web site provides two types of chart called "Quick Chart" and "Interactive Charting." After entering a stock symbol in the search slot and clicking on "Quick Chart," the trading data for the day is shown. Also available are a company or fund profile, analysts' ratings, insider transactions, and news on the company or fund. A one-year price and trading-volume chart is the main display on the home page.

By clicking on "Interactive Charting," you produce a menu on the left side of the screen. This menu allows you to construct a customized chart. You can select a time span from one day to 10 years, a particular year, or any other past time period. You can also compare the price performance of the stock or fund to several market indexes.

This site provides the capability for you to construct charts on stocks and funds with the characteristics you want, store those charts for reference later, and call them up when you return to the site. To activate this feature, scroll down the home page and watch the right side of the screen for "My Favorites" box. Click on "Chart Favorites." Then go to the left side of the screen to the interactive charting menu and construct the chart you want. After storing this chart you can return to it by way of the "My Favorites" box.

MSN MONEY WEB SITE

Web address: www.moneycentral.msn.com

The tool bar on the MSN Money home page lists "Investing" as a choice. Clicking on this selection generates a display titled "Market Dispatches," where the news on the stock market is presented. By scrolling down you also get news flashes on individual companies.

After reviewing those news items, you can then scroll back up and select "Stocks" from the tool bar. A display called "Welcome to Stock Research" appears. Here, under the heading of "Research Tools," you will find a proprietary service called "StockScouter." After entering a stock symbol in the search slot, click on "StockScouter," and a display of trading data on the subject stock for the day appears.

At the bottom of this display is a selection called "StockScouter Rating." Click on this, and a numerical rating on the stock is presented, with 1 being the lowest score and 10 the highest. Click on "StockScouter Rating" again and find a summary that indicates whether the stock is expected to outperform or underperform the market over the next six months. Also indicated is the level of risk in owning the stock.

To the right of the screen under the heading "Expected Risk/Return" is a comparison of risk to return shown by the lengths of the two bars representing each factor. This feature is unique to this site and is an objective assessment of a stock's levels of risk.

To get a detailed report on the fundamental condition and financial details on the company, use the following procedure.

At the home page enter the stock symbol.

To the right of the entry slot click on "Print Report."

A display from which you may select various types of fundamental financial data appears.

Select the information you want.

Scroll down to bottom of display and click on "Generate Report."

All the data and information you requested is printed out.

MARKETWATCH FROM DOW JONES

Web address: www.marketwatch.com

At the home page, click on "Investors' Tools" in the tool bar. This action presents choices of "Breaking News," "Interactive Charting," "Portfolio Tracking," and "Live Quotes." Click on "Interactive Charting" and enter a stock symbol in the search slot. Click on the arrow box and you will see the price change and volume of trading for the day. Also displayed is a one-year price and volume chart.

At the left of the screen is a menu for selecting a different time period from one day to five years for the chart. You can also compare the performance of the stock against the following indexes: Dow Jones Industrials, Standard & Poor's 500 Index, and the NASDAQ Index of 100 stocks. Under the heading "Indicators," you can display the earnings of the company, dividends paid, and stock splits. After choosing those display items, you can store them so they will be displayed again when you put another stock symbol in the search slot.

Returning to the home page, click on "Stocks" in the tool bar. Here you can get additional information, such as a profile of the business on any company, the latest news, insider trading, analysts' estimates of earnings, and financial statement.

QUANTUM ONLINE WEB SITE

Web address: www.quantumonline.com

This site provides information on a wide variety of securities and is one of the most comprehensive sources on preferred issues. For each preferred stock, it shows the price at the initial public offering, the amount of the dividend and whether it is cumulative, and the percentage of yield to the investor. It gives the call and maturity dates and the amount to be paid to the investor when the issue is called. It gives the credit ratings of the issue by Moody's Rating Service and Standard & Poor's to indicate the investment quality. It has a link to the listing stock exchange for a current price quote, volume of trading, the high and low prices during trading, and other data.

This site also provides lists of intital public offerings of preferred and common stocks, closed-end funds, real estate investment trusts, U.S. and Canadian royalty trusts, business development companies, preferred issues eligible for the 15 percent tax rate, and a screener that allows the investor to specify the attributes wanted in an investment. If you ever want to invest in preferred stocks or other specialized securities such as those mentioned above, this is an excellent starting point.

NATIONAL ASSOCIATION OF REITS WEB SITE

Web address: www.investinreits.com

This home page provides comprehensive educational information on real estate investment trusts (REITs), such as a "Guide to REIT Investing," "The REIT Story," "Glossary of REIT Terms," and how REITs are formed. It lists various types of REITs (e.g., residential, office buildings, shopping centers and malls, industrial parks, health-care facilities, hotels and other lodgings, mortgage securities, and public storage facilities). Some REITs own more than one type of property. Except for the mortgage securities REITs, all other REITs are based on the simple business model of owning real properties and collecting rents.

Click on "REITs by Ticker Symbol" on the home page and hundreds of REITs are listed by names and ticker symbols. To visit the Web site of a REIT, click on its name. To obtain information on the associated stock, click on its symbol. The display that comes up is the Yahoo! Finance page with the stock preselected. This screen provides the basic information, such as the volume of trading for the day, the average volume of trading for the preceding three months, the amount of the dividend and the percentage of yield, and the price-to-earnings ratio. This screen also provides a menu with links to technical information on the stock and fundamental data on the company.

Going back to the home page, the same information is available on REIT funds by clicking on "REIT Mutual Funds," "Closed-End Funds," and "Exchange-Traded Funds." This information is helpful to understanding REITs, and if you want to invest in them, this site is a good place to start your investigation.

SMART MONEY.COM WEB SITE

Web address: www.smartmoney.com

This home page displays a billboard of breaking news items and a feature article by a staff writer. On the left side of the screen is a menu with subjects such as stocks, funds, the economy, and articles from *Smart Money* magazine.

The best feature of this page is a watch list of 10 stocks that can be customized to show the investor's holdings. Clicking on a symbol in this list brings up a display containing a profile of each company, a chart of the day's stock price action, a summary of the trading data for the day, breaking news on the company, current and forecast earnings, and key statistics on each company's financial condition.

An investor can register with this Web site for additional services such as a portfolio tracker, a stock screener, performance data on particular businesses, and an update on the bond market and current interest rates.

D

BIBLIOGRAPHY

Darst, David M., *The Art of Asset Allocation*, New York: McGraw-Hill, 2003.

Edwards, Robert D., *Technical Analysis of Stock Trends*, 8th Ed., New York: St. Lucie Press, 2001.

Finn, Edward A. *Guide to Building Wealth*, New York: Barron's, 2000.

Jiler, William L., *How Charts Can Help You in The Stock Market*, New York: Trendline Publishing, 1962.

Meyer, Thomas A., *The Technical Analysis Course*, 3rd Ed., New York: McGraw-Hill, 2002.

Moglia, Joseph, *Coach Yourself to Success*, New York: John Wiley & Sons, 2005.

Murphy, John J., *Technical Analysis of Financial Markets*, New Jersey: Prentice Hall, 1999.

O'Neill, William J., *How to Make Money in Stocks*, New York: McGraw-Hill, 1988.

Pistolese, Clifford A., *Using Technical Analysis*, New York: McGraw-Hill, 1994.

Pring, Martin J., *How to Select Stocks Using Technical Analysis*, New York: McGraw-Hill, 2002

Tigue, Joseph, *Standard and Poor's Guide to Long-Term Investing*, New York: McGraw-Hill, 2003.

Weiss, Jeffrey, *Beat the Market*, New York: Cloverdale Press, 1985.

NOTE TO READER

I enjoyed writing this book. I hope you enjoyed reading it. Please answer the following questions and make any other comments.

1. What was the most helpful part of the book?
2. Which part needs improvement and how would you improve it?
3. Is there an area of technical analysis you would like to know more about?

Please send your comments to Cliffwrite@AOL.com. I do not open e-mail I don't recognize. Please use TA in the subject designation for the purpose of identification. Thank you for reading the book and for taking the time to comment.

Clifford Pistolese

ABOUT THE AUTHOR

Clifford Pistolese is the bestselling author of *Using Technical Analysis* and *Technical Analysis for the Rest of Us*. A successful trader, Pistolese has held executive positions with several Standard & Poor's 500 corporations.

INDEX

A/C, heating, and refrigeration, 81–82
A-list stocks, 16
Accumulation, 159
ACM Income Fund, 67
Active trading, 89
Aerospace/defense, 84
Affordable Residences, 49
Aggressive investing, 15–24
  (*See also* Bull market)
Agnico Eagle, 57
Akamai Technologies, 42
Allegheny Energy, 42, 158
Allegheny Technology, 46
Allied Capital, 46
Allied Waste, 84
Altria, 78
American Science, 76
American Standard, 82
American States Water, 75
Angle of ascent, 141, 169
Anglo Gold Ashanti, 57
Annual report, 159
Applix, 42
Aqua America, 66, 75
Arch Coal, 83
Archer-Daniels-Midland, 85, 158
Art Technology, 42
Assisted living, 75
Association of Closed-End Funds, 27,
  28
At the market, 90–91
Author's e-mail address, 183
Average trading volume, 159

Balanced style of investment, 25–31
  (*See also* Range-bound market)

Bank of South Carolina, 46
Barnes & Noble, 78
Barrick Resources, 57
Barron's, 26, 27, 36, 63
Bear market, 33–39
  chart, 6, 13
  defined, 6
  market tops, 34–35
  money market funds, 38
  municipal bonds, 36–37
  preferred stock, 37–38
  suggested portfolio mix, 38–39
  zero coupon bonds, 36
BHP Billiton, Ltd., 74
Bibliography, 181
Big Charts Web site, 175
Biotechnology companies, 81
Black & Decker, 81
Black Rock High Income, 50
BlackRock Global, 67
Boeing, 84
Bond:
  corporate, 63
  municipal, 36–37, 63
  zero coupon, 36
Bond funds:
  high-yield, 50
  tax-exempt, 49–50
Book publishers, 75–76
Books-A-Million, 78
Bookstores, 78
Borders, 78
Borrowing money, 90
Bottom fishing, 159
Bottoming out, 159–160
Bottoming pattern, 160

Breakout, 160
Broker:
  commission, 2
  conflict of interest, 1
  customer beware, 2
  discretionary account, 3
  finding one, 98–99
  Internet brokerages, 99–100
  investor's obligations, 100–101
  long-term relationships, 100–101
  solicitation calls, 92
  starting up, 99
Brookdale Senior Living, 75
Bull market, 15–24
  chart, 6, 13
  defined, 5
  end of, 34–35
  fundamental analysis, 23–24
  risk, 24
  starting up, 16–17
  stock prices and moving averages,
    17–23
  what to look for, 15–16
Bunge Ltd., 85
Burlington Northern, 83
Business model, 160
Businesses, types (see Types of
  business)
Buy and hold strategy, 69–86
  charts, 70–71
  following up, 85–86
  lists of companies (see Types of
    businesses)
  methodology, 72–73
  P/E ratio, 73–74
  stock selection, 69–71
Buying on margin, 160
Buying on tips, 91

California Pizza, 82
Call date, 160
Call price, 160
Cameco, 158
Canadian companies, 48–49, 83
Canadian Natural Resources, 83
Canon, 46
Canterra Gold, 57

Capital gain, 160
Capital gains (review exercise),
  103–118
Capital loss, 160
Capitulation, 160
Carolina Group, 78
Carpenter Tech, 158
Cascade Bancorp, 46
Cash flow per common share, 160
Casual dining, 80
Casual footwear manufacturers, 77
Casual Male Retail, 158
C.H. Robinson, 79
Chart patterns, 7–12
  double bottom, 10, 11
  double top, 8–9
  head and shoulders, 8
  inverted head and shoulders, 10
  pattern variations, 12
  rounding bottom, 10, 11
  rounding top, 8, 9
Churn an account, 161
Cigarette makers, 77
Citrix Systems, 42
CKE Restaurants, 80
ClearStation, 16, 173–174
Clorox Corporation, 74
Closed-end funds, 26–28, 62–63
Coal producers, 82–83
Colgate-Palmolive, 66, 74
Colonial High Income, 50
Commission, 2
Commodity prices, 35
Commodity Research Bureau Index
  (CRB), 35
Common stock, 161
Comtech Group, 42
Conagra, 85
Conflict of interest, 1
Consensus opinion, 93
Conservative investing (see Bear
  market)
Consolidated Energy, 83
Consolidation, 161
Continuation formation, 161
Corn Products, 79
Corporate bonds, 63

Courier Corp., 76
Covanta Holdings, 84
Cover a short sale, 161
Crane, 46
CRB, 35
Credit Suisse Group, 47
Credit Suisse High Yield, 50
CSX, 83
Cummins, 47
Cyanide heap leaching, 55
Cyclical industries, 35

Darden Restaurants, 80
Day trader, 161
Defense industry, 84
Defensive investing (*see* Bear market)
Defensive stocks, 161
Definitions (glossary), 159–170
Demand, 161
Discount, 161
Discount brokerage, 162
Discounted purchase price, 162
Discretionary account, 3, 162
Distribution, 162
Diversification, 61–67
   closed-end funds, 62–63
   index funds, 62
   money market funds, 64
   mutual funds, 62
   notes and bonds, 63
   precious metals, 64
      (*See also* Gold/gold-related
         investments)
   real estate, 63–64
   risk, 64–65
   sample portfolio, 66–67
   stocks, 61–62
      (*See also* Types of business)
Dividend, 162
Domino's Pizza, 80, 82
Double bottom, 10, 11
Double top, 8–9
Downside breakout, 162
Downtrend line, 162
Dreyfus High Yield, 50
Dril-Quip, 42, 158
Due diligence, 162

Eaton Vance Income Trust, 67
Eaton Vance Municipal Trust, 50
eBay, 66
Economic signs (end of bull market),
   35
Ediets.com, 77
El Paso, 80
Eldorado Gold, 57
Electric utilities, 79
Eltek, 42
Emerging markets, 162
Emotional reactions, 87–88, 94
Energizer Holdings, 74
Equity Residential Properties, 67
Exchange-traded gold funds, 54–55
Exchange-traded funds, 163
Exelon, 79
Exercises (*see* Review exercise)
Exploration Company of Delaware, 42
Exponential moving average, 12, 163
   (*See also* Stock prices and moving
      averages)

Fargo Electronics, 43
Faulty logic (*see* Pitfalls to avoid)
Fear, 94
FedEx, 47
finance.yahoo.com, 12, 23, 34, 42, 59,
   72, 85, 157, 172–173
First Cash Financial, 43
Flat liner, 88–89
Flowers Foods, 79
Food and drink companies, 79
Food products, 84–85
Freeport McMoran, 47, 57, 74
Frontier Oil, 47
Full-service broker, 1–3, 98–101, 163
   (*See also* Broker)
Fundamental analysis, 23–24
Fundamental information, 163
Futures market, 163

Garmin Ltd., 158
General obligation bond, 36
Genetech, 81
Gilead Sciences, 81
Glimcher Realty Trust, 49

Globalization, 163
Glossary, 159–170
Gold/gold-related investments, 53–59
    decision considerations, 58–59
    exchange-traded gold funds, 54–55
    gold bullion, 54
    hedging gold sales, 55–56
    lists of companies, 56–58
    mining, 55, 56
    risk, 56
    tracking your investment, 59
Gold bullion, 54
Gold mining, 55–58
Goldfields, Ltd., 57
Greed, 94
Growth company or fund, 163
Guess?, 43

Hain Celestial, 79
Harmony Gold, 57
Harsco, 47
Hawaiian Electric, 79
Head and shoulders, 8
Heating and air conditioning, 81–82
Hedging forward, 163
Hedging gold sales, 55–56
Hewlett-Packard, 47
High-income investments, 25–26,
    48–50
High-yield bond funds, 50
H.J. Heinz, 79
Homeland security, 76
Hope, 94
Household essentials, 80–81

Iam Gold, 57
Income-producing investments, 25–26,
    48–50
Index funds, 62
Indoor climate control, 81
Industry sectors (see Types of business)
Infosonics, 43
Initial public offering, 163–164
Intermediate term, 164
Intermediate-term winners, 46–48
Internet Web sites, 171–179
    (See also Web sites)

Inverted head and shoulders, 10
iShares Comex Gold, 54

J & J Snack Foods, 47
J.B. Hunt Transport Services, 79
JPMorgan Chase, 47

Key reversal day, 164
Kimco Realty, 47
Kinross Gold, 57
Kirby, 43

L–3 Communication, 76
Ladish, 43
Lease, 28
Lennox Intenational, 82
Limit order, 91, 164
Liquidation value, 164
Lockheed Martin, 84
Logitech International, 43
Long term, 164
Longevity of rise in price, 141
Lufkin Industries, 47

Manor Care, 47, 75
Margin account, 3
Margin call, 164
Market index, 164–165
Market phases, 5–7
Market tops, 34–35
MarketWatch from Dow Jones, 177
McGraw-Hill Companies, 76
Media hype, 91
Meridian Bioscience, 47
Meridian Gold, 57
Message board, 165
Message board comments, 93
Microcapitalized, 165
Middleby, 43
Mining companies, 55–58, 74
Mistakes to avoid (see Pitfalls to avoid)
Mobile Mini, 43
Momentum player, 165
Money market funds, 38, 64
Moody's Corporation, 165
Mortgage-backed securities, 165
Mossimo, 43

Moving average, 12
  (*See also* Stock prices and moving
    averages)
MSN Money Web site, 24, 48, 176
Municipal bonds, 36–37, 63
Municipal Holdings Fund, 50
Mutual funds, 62

NASDAQ, 165
National Association of REITs, 29,
  178–179
National Association of Securities
  Dealers, 99
Net asset value (NAV), 26
Newell Rubbermaid, 81
Newmont Mining Company, 57
Nike, 77
Nokia ADS, 47
Nondurable household products, 74
Norfolk Southern, 83
Northern Trust, 47
Northrop Grumman, 84
Note to reader, 183
Notes and bonds, 63
  (*See also* Bond)
Novartis AG, 81
Nursing homes, 75

Oakley, 43
Objective, 165
OGE Energy, 80
Oil and gas companies, 80, 83
Oil and gas royalty trusts, 50
One day reversal, 166
ONEOK, 80
Open pit mining, 55
Operating profit margin, 166
Ormat Technologies, 47
Overbought, 166
Overcommitting, 88
Oversold, 166

P/E ratio, 73–74, 166–167
Panera Bread, 79
Papa John's, 82
Paper loss, 166
Paper profit, 166

Par value, 166
Parabolic price curve, 22
Payless ShoeSource, 77
Peabody Energy, 83
Pearson plc, 76
Pengrowth Energy Trust, 49
Penny stocks, 90
PepsiCo, 66, 79
Petro-Canada, 83
Petrofund Energy Trust, 49
Picking winners, 41–51
  income-producing investments,
    48–50
  intermediate-term winners,
    46–48
  risk-return tradeoff, 48
  short-term winners, 42–45
PIMCO High Income, 50
Pioneer High Income, 50
Pitfalls to avoid, 87–95
  borrowing money, 90
  buying near the top, 88
  buying on the phone, 92
  buying on tips, 91
  buying what you don't understand,
    93–94
  consensus opinion, 93
  flat liner, 88–89
  media hype, 91
  message board comments, 93
  penny stocks, 90
  risk tolerance, 95
  rumors, 92–93
  selling short, 90
  tactical pitfalls, 88
  trading "at the market," 90–91
  trading emotionally, 94
  trading frequently, 89
  trading the tape, 89
Pizza companies, 82
Portfolio, 166
Practice exercises (*see* Review exercise)
Precious metals, 64
  (*See also* Gold/gold-related
    investments)
Preferred stock, 37–38
Premium price, 166

Preservation of capital, 35–38
  (*See also* Bear market)
Price charts (*see* Chart patterns)
Price/earnings (P/E) ratio, 73–74,
  166–167
Price increase (of stock), 141
Prime West Energy Trust, 49
Principal Financial Group, 47
Probable reserves, 167
Profit margin, 167
Prospectus, 167
Proven reserves, 167
Provident Energy Trust, 49
Public Storage, Inc., 78
Public storage facilities, 78
Pump and dump, 167

Quantum Online Web site, 37, 177–178

Railroad companies, 83
Randgold Resources, 57
Range-bound market, 25–31
  adjusting your portfolio, 25–26
  capital gains, 30–31
  chart, 7, 13
  closed-end funds, 26–28
  defined, 6
  REIT, 28–29
Raytheon, 84
Real estate, 63–64
Real estate investment trust (REIT),
  28–29, 49, 63–64, 178–179
Real estate investment trust funds, 29
Rebalance, 167
REIT, 28–29, 49, 63–64, 178–179
Relative strength, 167
Reliv International, 77
Republic Services, 84
Resistance level, 167
Restaurants, 80
Review exercise, 103–156
  capital gains, 103–118
  risk, 149–156
  stocks to avoid, 119–132
  time horizon, 141–148
  which stock has more potential?,
    133–140

Reynolds American, 78
Rio Tinto, plc, 74
Risk:
  bull market, 24
  gold, 56
  portfolio mix, 64–65
  review exercise, 149–156
  types of investments, 87
Risk aversion, 94, 168
Risk-return tradeoff, 48
Risk tolerance, 95
Rorschach test, 167–168
Rounding bottom, 10, 11
Rounding top, 8, 9
Royal Gold, 57
Royalty trusts, 49
RSA Security, 43
Rumors, 92–93

S&P 500 Index, 62, 164–165
S&P Midcap 400 Index, 62
S&P Smallcap 600 Index, 62
Salomon High Income II, 50
Sample stock portfolio, 157–158
Securities and Exchange Commission
  (SEC), 168
Selling short, 3, 90, 168
Service provider, 168
Shoe companies, 77
Short selling, 3, 90, 168
Short squeeze, 168
Short term, 168
Short-term winners, 42–45
Shurgard Storage, 78
Silver, 64
Simple moving average, 168
Skechers, 77
Smart Money.com Web site, 179
Smithway Motor Express, 43
Solicitation calls, 92
Sovran Storage, 78
Spot price, 168
SRA International, 76
Standard and Poor's Corporation, 169
Standard & Poor's 500 Index, 62,
  164–165
Starting up, 12–13

Stock Charts.com Web site, 174–175
Stock market phases, 5–7
Stock prices and moving averages:
    bull market, 17–23
    buy and hold, 70–71
    short-term winners, 44–45
Stock selection, 41–51
    (*See also* Picking winners)
Stockbroker, 1–3, 98–101
    (*See also* Broker)
Stocks to avoid (review exercise),
    119–132
Streaming quotes, 169
streetTRACKS Gold, 54, 67
Suncor Energy, 83
Sunrise Senior Living, 66, 75
Supply, 169
Support level, 169
Sustainable angle of ascent, 169
Swift Transportation, 79

Tax-exempt bond funds, 49–50
Technical analysis, 5, 169
Terminology (glossary), 159–170
Test yourself (*see* Review exercise)
TETRA Technologies, 43, 158
Thornburg Mortgage, 49
Time horizon (review exercise),
    141–148
Tips, 91
Tobacco products companies, 77–78
Topping and bottoming patterns
    (*see* Chart patterns)
Topping out, 169
Toyota Motors, 66
TradeStation Group, 43
Trading "at the market," 90–91
Trading on margin, 3
Trading platform, 169
Trading the tape, 89
Trailing stop loss order, 169
Transocean, 43
Transportation services, 79
TTM Technologies, 43
200-day exponential moving average, 12
    (*See also* Stock prices and moving
        averages)

TXU Corporation, 79
Types of business:
    A/C, heating, and refrigeration,
        81–82
    aerospace/defense, 84
    assisted living, 75
    biotechnology companies, 81
    book publishers, 75–76
    bookstores, 78
    Canadian companies, 83
    casual dining, 80
    casual footwear, 77
    coal producers, 82–83
    electric utilities, 79
    food and drink, 79
    food products, 84–85
    homeland security, 76
    household essentials, 80–81
    mining metals, 74
    natural gas producers, 80
    nondurable household products,
        74
    pizza companies, 82
    public storage facilities, 78
    railroad companies, 83
    tobacco products, 77–78
    transportation services, 79
    waste management, 84
    water utilities, 74–75
    weight control, 76–77

Underwrite, 169
Union Pacific, 83
United Technologies, 82
Upside breakout, 169–170
Uptrend line, 170
Utilities, 74–75, 79

VAALCO Energy, 43
Veritas DGC, 43

Waste Connections, 84
Waste Management, 84
Waste management companies,
    84
Water utilities, 74–75
WD–40 Company, 74, 158

Web sites, 171–179
   BigCharts, 175
   ClearStation, 173–174
   MarketWatch, 177
   MSN Money, 176
   National Association of REITs, 29,
      178–179
   Quantum Online, 177–178
   SmartMoney, 179
   StockCharts, 174–175
   Yahoo! Finance, 172–173
   (See also entries starting with www.)
Weight control companies, 76–77
West Pharmaceutical, 158
What not to do? (see Pitfalls to avoid)
Whirlpool, 81
Winning stocks (see Picking winners)
WPCS International, 43
www.bigcharts.com, 175
www.cefa.com, 27, 28
www.clearstation.com, 16, 173–174

www.crbtrader.com, 35
www.investinREITS.com, 29,
   178–179
www.kitco.com, 54
www.marketwatch.com, 177
www.moneycentral.msn.com, 24, 48,
   176
www.NASD.com, 99
www.quantumonline.com, 37,
   177–178
www.smartmoney.com, 179
www.stockcharts.com, 174–175
www.treasurydirect.gov, 36

Yahoo! Finance Web site, 12, 23, 34, 42,
   59, 72, 85, 157, 172–173
Yamana Gold, 57
Yield, 170
York Water, 75

Zero coupon bond, 36, 170